Unwrapped

The Pursuit of Justice
for Women Educators

KENDRA WASHINGTON-BASS, PhD
and KELLY PEAKS HORNER, MEd

CONTENTS

Tandem Light Press
950 Herrington Rd.
Suite C128
Lawrenceville, GA 30044

Tandem Light Press paperback edition Autumn 2022

ISBN: 978-1-7376438-6-9

PRINTED IN THE UNITED STATES OF AMERICA

This book is dedicated to the countless women who have continued to chip away at the glass ceiling and create their own arenas for us to flourish and thrive. We stand on your shoulders and hope to continue to pave the way for other women educational leaders.

For my mother, Karen, my grandmother, Barbara, my great-grandmother, Vivian, and my great-great-grandmother, Helen. I say your names and lift you up because I am because you are.

Thank you.

KWB

This book is dedicated to the women, all women, who start as allies and listen to learn, grow into accomplices to stand together, and emerge as coconspirators willing to risk their privilege in order to create systems where all women belong and thrive.

For the women education leaders who have served as an example of courage, accountability, and generosity, who introduced me to the words "If not me, then who?" and to the women in my life now who challenge me to be my best, be better, and continue this work.

I am grateful.

KPH

ACKNOWLEDGMENTS

We could not have written this book without the countless family, friends, and colleagues who have encouraged us throughout the years. We recognize that this book is a culmination of people, events, and situations that have shaped who we are today. We want to acknowledge that we appreciate the learning from all who have impacted our lives.

We would like to give special thanks and acknowledgment to the following people who have poured into us and brought this work to life: Karen Washington, Jason Bass, Justice Bass, Julian Bass, Barbara Chappell, Cynthia Brown, Brenda Kemp, Denise Kemp, Tracey Geiger, Kimberly Nelson, Roxanne Griffin, Kevin Kemp, Phyllis Kemp, Darren Kemp, Sonia Kemp, Bernadette Payne, Kimberly Davis, Anita Bryant, Amy Dryer Rodriguiz, Charisse Gibbs, Maria Liu Wong, Michelle Johnson Kelly, Ivelisse Nunez, Rochelle Valsaint, Iris Outlaw, Dr. Glenn Pethel, Linda Daniels, Dr. Charisse Redditt, Dr. Erin Hahn, Eliana Pereyra, Lisa Adkisson, Dona Smith, Tonya Robinett, Raquel Gonzalez, Jennifer Peterson, Dr. Michelle Farmer, Dr. Chandra Walker, Monica Rosen, Dr. Dionne Cowan, Dr. Crystal Cooper, Margaret Ackerman, Maryanne Grimes, Vivian Stranahan, Cindy Truett, Susan Smith, Halima Gray, Valerie Lewis, Berthine Crevecoeur West, Dr. Frances Davis, Dr. Monica Batiste, Dr. Kelli McCain, Dr. Tonya Burnley, Socorro Santos-Winters.

Steve Horner, Madi Horner, Shelby Horner, Mary Lou Peaks, Jami Bailey, Michael Peaks, Rose Horner, Mary Mance, Dr. Kerry

Robinson, the brilliant women of the 2019 Women Leading Women Conference at the University of Nottingham, Brené Brown, BBERG, and the Dare To Lead Facilitators, Sister Mary Donna, Mary Hatwood Futrell, Betsy Arons, Linda Goldberg, Kay Eckler, Jane Woods, Jewel Purdy DeVries, Mary Kay Prioletti, Wendy Sanback Van Stee, Tony Nocera, Joyce Wells, Suzie Sterrett, Dr. "Bud" Spillane, Dr. Alan Leis, Dr. Brad Draeger, and all those who influenced my teaching, Maureen Daniels, Rick Willis, Dr. Denny Dunkley, Roseanne Liesveld, Gary Gordon, Nancy Oberst, Glenn Pethel, Frances Davis, Sid Camp, Kathy Geiger, Debbie Terry, Angela Bain, Angela Smith, Nancy Graham, Dana Krizar, Dionne Cowan, participants in the many cohorts of Dare to Lead™ education leaders, Washington & Kemp "Zoom" Family, and all the incredible yoga instructors I have had the honor to share space with and who have taught me the meaning of being present.

We are grateful for Tandem Light Press: Dr. Pamela Larde, Caroline Smith, Lee Ashby Watts, and Djemie Maurancy. Thank you for being the women we needed. You pushed us to think deeper about the message of the work we will do to positively impact the lives of women in leadership. Your guidance, advice, and care for our very personal work are greatly appreciated.

Lastly, we want to thank the countless people, experiences, and friendships that have shaped our work. We are especially grateful for our friendship that has developed into a sisterhood. The evolution of our sisterhood was the impetus to write this book. Two text messages: "Want to write a book about women in educational leadership?" "Yes." And the story began to be written. Instinct, faith, trust, and God's guidance have led us here. The journey has been fun and difficult at times. We look forward to creating our arena and together becoming unwrapped.

INTRODUCTION
STORIES MATTER

Many stories matter. Stories have been used to dispossess and to malign. But stories can also be used to empower, and to humanize. Stories can break the dignity of a people. But stories can also repair that broken dignity.

— Chimamanda Ngozi Adichie

EVERY WOMAN LEADER has a story. The stories of triumph, heartbreak, persistence, resilience, and failure are the best data we have to examine our social conditioning and how we need to break free from it. Stories show what is missing, what is real, what is predominant. Over the past decade, women have been taking hold of their power. We can feel it and see it from the Me Too movement, #TimesUp, to the 2020 vice presidential nominee's declaration "I am speaking!" We have had it. There is beginning to be a shift in how we lead, and we are not apologizing for it.

So how did we get here and what do we do now? If we are to ever move the needle and own the narrative, we have to start with telling our stories and healing ourselves. We have to unwrap the layers of anger, misogyny, societal norms, stereotypes, sexism, gendered racism, and self-imposed and collective shaming that have kept us from thriving. A powerful lever we have at our disposal is our educational system. We can use it to shape the lives of young girls and boys so that they do not perpetuate the isms that continue to "place" people in society.

And yet the story of women in educational leadership is both disturbing and fascinating. The number of women in senior leadership positions in schools and districts has not changed much since the late 1990s. Oh sure, we have made some progress. But when we consider that nearly 80 percent of women make up the teaching force and only 33 percent of women are in the top-tier leadership positions within their districts, we know that there is a problem. And when distilling the numbers further by race, the numbers are appalling, with only 5 percent of Black women leading school districts.

We aren't doing nearly enough. It's time to explore what's missing and identify strategies and tools to address the gaps. This book is about helping us unwrap ourselves to learn who we are, how we show up, and what we do to support each other to lead with courage, resilience, and authenticity.

In 2008, our career paths crossed and we, in our separate, parallel ways, have been coaching, training, and supporting school leaders to build the capacity of the teachers and administrators they serve. We are passionate about growing educators, and we are especially passionate about developing leaders. As we remained connected through the years, we began to notice a pattern in our work. Schools and districts were promoting leaders who did not look like the diverse children they served, and female leaders, especially women of color, were disproportionately overlooked in senior-level positions. As we listened to their stories, we began to notice similar trends, women being passed over for district-level promotions in favor of White male leaders with less experience, women placed in "challenging" positions and schools with very little support, and narrowed, purposeful leadership experiences for women, pigeon-holing them to specific roles and duties.

These experiences led to a deeper examination of the training and support that is developed and provided to women educational leaders. But most importantly, it led to our own self-examination. What we realized was that many of the strategies and tools to navigate these spaces safely are scarce for women in the leadership pipeline. In fact, as we examined our own development, we learned that our stories are not unique. We shared many of the challenges that we heard and witnessed from our sisters in the work. Our conditioning and wrapping meant that we would remain the nurturers, peacemakers, and workhorses, while our male counterparts were the decision-makers and managers. These characteristics were lauded as prerequisite skills an educational leader should possess. And when a woman dared to be decisive, confident, or fierce, then we were immediately deemed too strong, angry, mean, or worse—preventing hiring managers and school boards from considering women in top-tier leadership positions.

We have decided to write this book because we want to tell our story. We want to unwrap the layers of conditioning that form our journeys. We start with our own unique origin stories. Through our stories, we will share our personal conditioning, our teaching—informal and formal, our leading, and our unlearning to learn. We expose our conditioning as a way to illustrate the White male patriarchal lens we navigate and, in some instances, perpetuate. For the purposes of this book, we explore how race and gender intersect in our lives and how we each navigate them toward coconspiratorship. As we discuss race, we will primarily discuss the Black experience, and when we discuss gender, we are primarily sharing the female experience in educational leadership and the workforce. We acknowledge the stories of other marginalized voices are important to tell. It is not our place to speak for those communities. However, all stories of voices that have been silenced within the school systems should and must be told. We will lean on the over twenty-five years of experience and research we have conducted to share how our well-being is impacted when we do not have the systems of support in place to thrive. Additionally, we will use our expertise to shine a light on moments when we have to be courageous to get what we want and deserve.

We don't purport to know the answers to the gender and race issues, nor do we purport that the stories we share are shared by all women, most women, and Black women. Our hope is that our stories spark your own learning, self-discovery, reflection, and action to make a positive difference in your life and the women you work, play, and live with. We also hope that you begin to unwrap your layers of learning to discover how you have navigated your leadership journey so that you can begin to free yourself and be unapologetically you.

KELLY'S ORIGIN STORY
THE PEACEKEEPER AND PRETTY PRESENTS

When women are the storytellers the human story changes.
— Elizabeth Lesser

MY STORY BEGINS at the end. I have experienced many crossroad moments in my life. I would soon learn the decision I was about to make would be the fork in the road toward a new path I didn't know I was searching for and would reveal an exciting new direction and partnership. I learned all I had done and all I had learned was leading up to this moment. What I know now is it was the culmination of all my life experiences that led me down this road, and that realization is nothing short of life-changing.

On June 6, 2016, after nearly sixteen years doing a job I loved, I made the arduous decision to leave my employer and the culture where I could no longer thrive. I loved the work I was doing as a senior development consultant in the Education Practice at Gallup, an international research and consulting company. I loved my school partners, truly loved them, and was energized by their life's mission to make days at school and on campus better for students, teachers, and staff. I had been working with many of these genuinely gifted and courageous leaders during my entire tenure at Gallup. When I would visit with them and spend time white-boarding plans, ideas, and imagining how school for students and staff might be different, it was like visiting with family. We built trusting relationships that made tackling their greatest challenges together an honor. They considered me a confidante and trusted advisor. In one district just north of Atlanta, I was presented with a polo shirt just like the one their HR team wears when recruiting and hosting training events. I was a member of the team and one of them. To be clear, I was not leaving them. I was leaving the job, my employer, and the culture that no longer allowed me to thrive and do my very best work.

It was not always that way. After all, I remained in my position for nearly sixteen years. Board decisions and changes in how we were to do business, a flat organizational design, and the embedded misogyny and favoritism forced too many colleagues to hustle for acceptance and created a culture of unhealthy competition—always striving to be perfect and align oneself to power—and shame. The board determined the company would shift most of its focus from consulting to training and product sales. The measurable outcomes for consultants became how many butts you could get in training seats. I watched many long-time, well-respected leaders within the company leave. I chalked it up to avoidance of change or, as Angela Duckworth teaches, a closed mindset. I told myself they were stuck in nostalgia and wanted things to remain the way they had always been. They were simply disgruntled, afraid of a new way of doing business, and afraid of losing their positions of power and authority. A year after the board made this calculated decision, I realized it was more than just the avoidance of change. The decision to relinquish their positions after being top of their game was courageous. They weren't afraid of change at all. Rather, they remained aligned with their values. I have also grown to understand that our team structure was intentionally designed to center, support, and promote a mediocre White man who, based on my experience working closely with him, was not qualified for the specific job and title he was gifted. All the projects I created, sold, and managed were to be designed to cater to this man. The default, if it was not him, was the "cool kids" who aligned themselves with the powerful "legacy" leaders. What I understand now is I was working at the apex of patriarchy and favoritism. And it's when I began to dismantle that structure that my troubles began.

I have struggled with telling my story for several years. Best-selling author Glennon Doyle in her book, *Untamed,* talks about how women are tamed and socialized to move through the world. I was tamed early on to be the peacekeeper. I was conditioned to be the one who kept everything afloat and the waters calm, keep myself and my voice small and quiet and make sure everyone else is uplifted, happy, and thriving. I was raised in a fairly traditional household. We weren't well off, but we wanted for little. I would learn later that finances were always a struggle even though we always had our needs met and my parents chose to send my brother, sister, and me to Catholic schools. This could not have been financially easy for them.

My dad was loving and kind but also a man of his generation and southern upbringing. He was born and raised in deep south Mississippi. My parents lived in that small rural town for a short time, approximately two years. Most families were somehow involved in farming including my uncle, aunt, and cousins. They worked the family farm. Growing up, we rarely visited the small rural town where my dad grew up. And my grandparents visited us just once at our home in Virginia. But the few memories I have of the times we did are pretty vivid. My grandparents worked for the largest nursery and greenhouse owner in town. My grandmother managed the office, and my grandfather supervised the farms and laborers.

My clearest and most significant memory of visiting my grandparents was when I was just starting high school. I was intrigued by the contrast between our life in suburban Virginia and that of the rural life and community where my father was raised. I loved waking to the smell of my grandmother's homemade biscuits, and when they were hot out of the oven lathering on homemade jam and sitting down to eat at the petite kitchen table that was set in a small nook in her tiny kitchen. My grandfather would take us with him to check on crops and the farmworkers. And when we were done, we would stop by the small general store owned and operated by the nursery proprietor where my grandmother managed his business. At the store, we would always get treated to a straight from the cooler, small green-glass bottle of Coca-Cola.

On this specific visit, I remember the first time witnessing the vast disparities in how members of this same community lived in the south. There were shacks, literally shacks, where the Black farm workers lived. And I recall the jolt that shot through my body when I heard people we encountered, including family, use the N-word. I remember being startled to hear someone use it in casual speech and not in a movie or music video. I had never heard my dad speak this way. So it was breathtaking when I heard those he called friends and family do so. Perhaps the difference was my dad left that town right after college to join the Marine Corps. And he never returned except for an occasional visit.

This was my first clear memory and real encounter with overt racism, racist language, and a culture where both were commonly accepted and unnerved very few. I didn't fully understand the depth of what I saw and heard, and it would be much later in my life when I began my own antiracism unwrapping that I would come to fully understand and come to terms with what I had seen and witnessed while visiting family.

My dad believed his familial responsibility was to go to work, bring home a paycheck, and provide food and shelter for his family. He would return home after a long day, enjoy a wonderful home-cooked meal, and then retire with a book. He was a voracious reader. When he couldn't find a book lying around the house, any book, he would grab an edition of the Funk & Wagnall's Encyclopedia mom purchased with points she earned buying our groceries at the local supermarket. My mother's role was that of cook, housekeeper, and attendant to most of the needs of the children.

There were three children in our family—me, my younger sister, and my older brother. I was the middle child. My brother and I were very close growing up primarily due to being only a year and a half apart in age. My sister and I had more time and distance between us, being six years apart. Unlike my brother, we did not experience life's milestones together. We were never in the same school, hung out with the same friends, nor did we have similar interests at the same time. It wasn't until we were both married that we had a life experience in common. And when we both had children, we raised them together and created very close cousin ties.

My mom was a nontraditional woman of her time as she also worked outside the home. That was how she always moved through her world. I always wondered how she felt about the two years she lived in that small, rural town in Mississippi. The contrast between how my mom and dad grew up could not have been greater. Mom grew up in a small city-like town outside of Pittsburgh, Pennsylvania. My grandparents' home stood right on Main Street. I also loved visiting there, as it was so dissimilar to our home. We visited my mom's childhood home and my grandmother often.

My mom's dad passed away in 1971. I don't have very many memories of him, only stories I heard from my mom and her sisters. I remember the apartment where mom grew up having a long central hallway that flowed from the outdoor balcony that looked over Main Street to the entry of the large, blue dining room. The dining room held a substantial table that was perfect for holding all the diverse dishes neighbors would bring whenever there was an occasion to celebrate or death to mourn. The rooms were large. My favorite being the immense pink bathroom with the stand-alone tub. Her home was positioned above an "old-fashioned" drug store. Not a drug store like the CVS or Walgreens we know today. This was the local drug store that served the entire community. You could go there to get the medicines you needed, as well as, a drink from the soda fountain.

When mom was growing up, as she tells it, she would stop downstairs for a malt or cream soda before going upstairs to do her homework. Mom's hometown was a diverse, blue-collar town located adjacent to a US steel mill factory. Most everyone in town was either an employee of the mill or lived with someone who worked there. It was a town of immigrants from Croatia, Italy, and Poland. There was a vibrant Black community that lived in a section of town called Lincoln Way. Ironic, I know. Mom describes very few racial issues that occurred while growing up there. However, Blacks and Whites went to school together and returned home to their segregated neighborhoods. There might not have been any visible or physical tensions, but that might have been because everyone "knew their place."

Mom rose early every morning, helped get us off to school, then put on her brown collate restaurant uniform and apron and walked up the big hill to the steakhouse where she cooked and served customers for eight hours to contribute financially to our household. When my parents had occasions to celebrate with each other, such as Christmas, birthdays, and anniversaries, I was the one who reminded my dad to purchase a gift for my mom. He would give me cash, and I would walk to the local mall to purchase her something nice, something I thought she might like and that he might like to give her. I would wrap it in beautiful wrapping with a bow on top. My dad would present it to her with pride.

And it kept the peace. After all, I was the middle child. It was in my birth order to be the peacekeeper. I played this role well and I played it behind the scenes. I didn't make a fuss. I never revealed who actually did the labor of walking to the mall, deciding what to purchase, and creating the pretty present she was about to open. Although, I think mom knew and was ok with it. I kept quiet. I kept small. I did the work and allowed my dad to be on the metaphorical stage.

This was a role I would take on in so many ways at work, at home, and in relationships. I would create and provide opportunities for others to be on stage and present their gifts. I would do the labor to create opportunities for others to shine and receive accolades. And after over six decades of serving in this life role, I grew tired. I became resentful. And I had enough of showing up compliant, small, and quiet. I wanted to shed that role of peacekeeper. I no longer want to assimilate to what a family or misogynistic corporate culture expects or mandates of me and to instead show up as my one true, authentic self, create the healthy boundaries I need, and live and lead into my values.

The research on birth order and years separating siblings reveals that if there is more than a three- or four-years difference, it's like raising two distinct families. That is how it felt growing up. My sister and I being six years apart in age and my brother and I being so close in age felt often like two different family experiences. My brother and I attended high school together. Our graduating classes were just two years apart. My sister and I never attended school at the same time. My brother and I attended the same college. I graduated and started my teaching career before my sister began her post-secondary studies.

But where our experience was identical was in how we developed our work ethic. My varied and lengthy job experience started when I was in the eighth grade. I attended St. Agnes Elementary School, a K–8 Catholic school in Arlington, Virginia. The parish rectory was looking for a receptionist on Saturdays. They needed someone who would greet visitors, answer phone calls and take messages for the parish priests, collate the Sunday bulletins, and distribute them in the church ready for Sunday mass. My mom was best friends with the weekday receptionist, so I had an ally and a connection. I began working every Saturday throughout my eighth-grade year. As I got to know the full-time cook who prepared meals for the priests in residence, I was eventually asked to fill in for her when she was away. At the young age of fifteen, I was managing the parish rectory alone on Saturdays and cooking for the priests on occasion. From time to time my friends would come by to visit on their bikes. I was so envious of their freedom from responsibility on our day off from school. I was, however, able to contribute financially. It kept the peace when I would ask or need something and could afford to buy it. I could tie my needs up in a pretty package with a bow. I had a job. This experience also began my uninterrupted history of work.

I don't remember being without a job except for a brief time after I left Gallup. My siblings and I worked from when we were in late elementary and middle school. My sister started her work history at a Catholic retreat center. She helped out in the kitchen and with various tasks preparing for and during retreat events. My brother had a paper route where he delivered papers on his bike every afternoon and eventually began teaching tennis lessons at a local tennis club. We both spent many years working for our community recreation department as camp counselors, fitness instructors, gym attendants, and front desk workers. During college, I worked in the cafeteria and put up with catcalls, heckling, and unwanted advances from the university cafeteria manager. This was one of my first memories of experiencing misogyny and White male-dominated power. I put up with it as I needed the job to pay my school expenses. I laughed it off or ignored it to "keep the peace."

I can't remember taking a full winter break or summer off without working. During winter breaks from college, I worked for an inventory company and spent long days and hours counting stock products, merchandise, and supplies. Just imagine the tedium required to count nails, bolts, and screws at a hardware store! Summers were spent making telephones on an assembly line for Western Electric. I don't mean smartphones. I am talking about obsolete and archaic rotary phones. My brother and I both worked at the factory. We felt as though we'd hit the jackpot with this particular job as we were paid union wages even though we were summer help. Now, "the jackpot" in the early 80s was $14 an hour. That was unheard of for a part-time summer job. This particular opportunity allowed us to pay our college expenses and complete our degrees.

Immediately after graduating with my undergraduate degree in elementary education, I began my teaching career as an elementary teacher with Fairfax County Public Schools (FCPS). I loved teaching. I loved my students. I loved the other teachers who taught alongside me. In my first teaching assignment as a second-grade teacher, I taught next door to a first-grade teacher who was also very active in the political and advocacy side of the profession. Jane became a mentor to me, and I cherished our discussions about how we could make the profession better and support teachers in doing their job to make a greater impact on students. I was intrigued by how critical decisions were made, really made, and how policy was created. She stirred the activist in me I never knew was there.

One afternoon, she invited me to attend a teachers' association meeting with her. This particular group lobbied and petitioned the state for what schools and districts needed to improve working conditions, salaries, and instruction. This committee of engaged and dedicated classroom educators worked to influence policy and create meaningful change. I was hooked. I went back the next week and the next week. I became an activist for the profession. Over time, I met with local, state, and national elected officials to discuss much-needed changes in education. I served on various local, state, and national committees, and was elected to represent the teachers in my building. I allowed my name to be used as the litigant in a lawsuit against the school district suing to overturn the school board's decision to freeze salaries. The association needed a single litigant and I agreed partly in order to "keep the peace."

In 1991 I was serving on the Fairfax Education Association (FEA) board of directors when I was approached by the president-elect to consider running to be the next president. I was stunned. After all, I was barely thirty years old and had only seven years of experience in the classroom. The board was made up of individuals with much more experience. Most board members had been teaching for more than fifteen years. Collectively they possessed a deep history of the Association and experience in activism. After several conversations, I launched a campaign for president with the slogan, "The Future Is Now!" I thought that would address concerns about my youth and minimal experience. I won my election and, in 1992, began serving as president of FEA. This was the awakening of my lifelong activism, in general, and in education, specifically. It pushed me to the "edge of my becoming," as Sue Monk Kidd so eloquently writes. Activism and working to make this world better, or at least to create better days at school for both teachers and students, felt right. It was like a symbolic place to call home that I would later board up in order to fit in.

Before taking office, I married my best friend, Steve. I was navigating a new married life along with the responsibilities of the office. Steve works in government service and has a job that takes him overseas quite often. I missed him when he was gone, although it gave me the time I needed to navigate my official responsibilities without the guilt society places on us when not being at home and caring for others. Later, we would laugh about having been married five years and only seen each other for two of them. But it worked. We made time when we were able and treated the reprieves in his travel as honeymoons. My need for compliance, planning, and peacekeeping had me manifest a life plan where I would be pregnant with my first child during my last year in office and immediately go out on maternity leave. Every time I shared my plan with other women, they laughed and told me how it doesn't always happen that way. Well, it did. Even my body wanted to keep the peace. I delivered our first daughter, Madison, two weeks before the end of my president's term. I delivered my final speech before the school board only days after leaving the hospital. The school board meetings in Fairfax were televised, and Madi, as we call her, was introduced to the community on air. My tenure as president was another crossroads in my career. I would never return to the classroom.

I clearly remember one day while being on maternity leave, sitting in the parking lot of our local grocery store. Steve, Madi, and I made a quick stop for a few items. Steve went in to retrieve what we needed while I remained in the car to care for and entertain our daughter. At that moment sitting in the car, an overwhelming feeling of sadness, grief and gloom came over me. I could not get the mental movie out of my head of Madi needing me one day, for something, for anything, and not being there for her. I began to cry that ugly cry. When Steve returned to the car with our food items he was shaken upon seeing me.

"What happened?" he yelled and began to look around for anyone who might have caused us harm.

I screamed out, "I can't leave her alone." He was confused. I told him about sitting in the car, laughing and baby talking with her, and the mental movie playing in my head. I told him I wanted to figure something out where I could stay home with her a little longer, contribute financially to our household, and make a plan to return to the district when she was a little older. I knew being able to contribute financially was a way to get what I needed and keep the peace. My husband is an amazing provider and partner and sees so much of life through financial well-being. He lives with the value of building and maintaining our wealth for the future. By working hard now and making sacrifices in order to live an abundant retirement life. Steve saw on my face I was not asking for permission, but, rather, sharing with him what was going to happen and asking for his help to make it a reality. I would delay returning to the district and begin to craft a plan on how to make money. This decision was my entryway into entrepreneurship. I created ABC Tutoring Co. I worked with enough students every week to allow me to help pay bills and stay home with Madi.

About a year into being home and growing my business, I was contacted by the assistant superintendent of FCPS's human resource department. My time at FEA allowed me to make connections and create relationships throughout the school system. These connections allowed for some nontraditional ways of working for the district. Brad explained they were implementing a new interview process for teacher applicants, and with my being a teacher leader, he wanted to know if I would be interested in becoming one of the interviewers. They would provide the training and support necessary, the interviews would be conducted by phone, and I would complete them all from home. I think all I heard in this initial conversation was that I could work from home. By this time, I was pregnant with our second daughter, Shelby, and I knew I wanted to stay home with her as Madi prepared to start preschool. That meant I needed to figure out how to increase my financial contribution to our family.

I immediately said, "I'm in." Not knowing what this was about, I attended the first training. The superintendent was present as well as consultants and trainers from the Gallup Organization. What I discovered during the training was that the district contracted with Gallup to create an interview specifically for FCPS that would correlate to the behaviors and talents of the very best teachers in the district and provide insight into applicants who had the potential to perform just like them. The research and data were fascinating, the training was exceptional, and the purpose behind the interview spoke to my mission. The district was committed to putting the most talented teachers in front of students. Thus began my long relationship with the Gallup Organization.

Over the next several years I worked inside the district to coordinate the interview process, improve the quality of interview results, and serve as the direct contact to our Gallup partners. I created best practices to sustain both the reliability and validity of the interview results. I was asked by Gallup consultants to share my initiatives and practices with other HR leaders around the country.

I loved the mission behind the work of recruiting, assessing, and hiring the very best teachers. As I interviewed them, I imagined how they would create amazing learning experiences at school for their students and how I would feel if this candidate became my Madi or Shelby's teacher.

In April of 1999, Steve accepted a job that required us to move to Miami, Florida. My HR supervisor at FCPS asked if I would consider staying on as a consultant for the district and continuing with the recruitment and interviewing of teacher applicants. At that time, Fairfax would receive thousands of applicants and needed to quickly assess their strengths and fit for the district. I agreed and off we went to Florida. Once we got settled, I began to recruit at local job fairs and interview applicants from Florida who applied to the district. I guess you could say I was one of the early virtual workers for a school district before it was a thing and before districts were thrust into creating a new way of delivering instruction due to the pandemic.

Since I was a consultant with the district and not a full-time employee, nothing prevented me from doing other work. Gallup called. I agreed to another consulting contract where I would work in partnership with a current Gallup employee. Eventually, after I learned all I needed to know I would be able to work solo, and I would consult with the districts in Florida that collaborated with the company. If I met mutually defined metrics set up for my performance, I would have the option to go full-time. I moved between the two consulting contracts daily and loved the work both afforded me while also working to establish a new life for my family in a state I was totally unfamiliar with.

On September 11, 2001, at 8:46 a.m., I was watching *The Today Show* while preparing my interviews for the day. I watched Katie Couric and Matt Lauer interrupt the show and announce that an

American Airlines Boeing 767 had hit the north tower of the World Trade Center in New York City. I called Steve at work to share the news that there had been a tragic plane crash. I explained that it had hit the north tower of the World Trade Center. Eighteen minutes later, the second plane, a Boeing 767, United Airlines Flight 175, hit the south tower. I screamed into the phone. Steve seemed to know immediately what was happening.

As the morning progressed, I stayed glued to the news. I heard the report at 9:45 a.m. American Airlines Flight 77 had just crashed into the west side of the Pentagon. This shook me to my core as we had just moved from the DC metro area and still had family and friends in the area. Many worked in the city, and some worked at the Pentagon. I frantically called my mom to discover if she was still at work in the city and whether she was on the move to return home safely. There was mass confusion at her job around what to do in order to keep their employees safe. I remember telling my mom to go home now as it might be just a matter of time before transportation out of the city was shut down, and if there is another attack, it might be on bridges, and she might be trapped. She assured me she would pack up her things and head home immediately.

As my mom and I were talking, the news reported that at 10:10, United Flight 93 was hijacked and later crashed in an open field near Shanksville in western Pennsylvania. I knew Steve was right. These were not just coincidental horrific crashes. This was something more. That evening when Steve arrived back home, we began our discussion about returning to the metro area. Within a few months, we were packing up and returning to Washington, DC, and Steve would return to the work that allowed him to live out his mission and purpose of serving and protecting our country.

Upon arrival back in Virginia, I received two job offers. I was asked to return to FCPS and become the director of recruitment.

And since I met all my consulting benchmarks with Gallup, I was asked to join the education practice full time. I chose Gallup. The work allowed me to meet with school district leaders all over the country and solve problems together that were unique to their districts and communities. At this crossroads, I walked away from Fairfax County Public Schools permanently but would forever take the thirteen years of varied experiences with me wherever I went. As I embarked on my career at Gallup I discovered many school leaders had some experience or affiliation with FCPS. My affiliation and history with the district served me well in my new role. It made creating relationships so much easier. There was an instant connection.

The work I was doing in the Education Practice felt just like discovering those phenomenal teachers who had the potential to change the lives of their students. When I facilitated professional development with principals and talked about the most important aspect of their job, hiring talented teachers, that same feeling resonated when the light bulb came on and they realized it was about more than just what was on the resume. I knew I was making an impact on students through those principals. And I was able to affect district processes and practices all over the country.

My work progressed over sixteen years and included partnerships with district leaders at all levels. The goal? Create better days for students by creating better cultures and conditions for adults. A few years before deciding to leave Gallup, our Education Practice experienced a very significant leadership change. The leadership within the team shifted, and our work was assimilated into the collective community of the company. I was excited. As a senior consultant and project manager, I now had the opportunity to work with a larger team of researchers, trainers, thought leaders, and content specialists. I was impatient to introduce them to my clients and partners. I was confident we would be able to make a greater impact on the daily lives of students and teachers and would be able to break new ground in research around what really matters to make schools thrive.

In this moment of change, two mindsets were dominating our team, one of growth, excitement, and curiosity about the future and one of closed, self-preservation, how-will-this-affect-me rumination. I was in the first group. I didn't see what the other group was about to do. I didn't see them coming.

I began to schedule meetings with some of the best research and strategic minds at the company and we engaged in intellectual, innovative discussions about how to realign our current work, what else do we want to know, what don't we know, and how to best build and expand client teams. I communicated to colleagues and team members that I would reach out to new ways of thinking and if they would be patient, we would have consequential projects to work on with an expanded internal partner team to deliver results for our district partners. I was excited to go to work every day and discover how we could take research that was being conducted in other areas of the company and apply it to schools.

One Saturday morning in May 2014, I received an email that would create another crossroads moment for me. It was a beautiful cool-temperatures spring morning. I had just finished my morning walk on the Washington & Old Dominion Trail (W&OD). The W&OD is a paved trail that runs for forty-five miles along the former roadbed of the Washington & Old Dominion Railroad. The trail runs through rural Virginia and will take you into the city of Washington, DC. There was an entry point to the trail near our home. I was enjoying my second-morning coffee to take a bit of the chill off and texting with a good friend. I opened the email from one of my former supervisors. She wasn't just any supervisor but one who had a great deal of power throughout the company. She was a member of the family that held great power, ownership, and control over the organization from the inside. She was a "legacy." Several of our team members aligned themselves closely with her and worked overtime to gain her favor. And there were a few who developed such personal relationships with her that they were almost like family. I did not interact with her much at this time but was invited to join her and some of her new team for lunch a few days prior to receiving her email. She asked a lot of questions about what I was working on, who I was working with, and what my goals were for the year. I enthusiastically and vulnerably shared how I was working with some of the researchers we had not worked with in the past on realigning our work to create greater opportunities for districts and greater impact. I named the names of people I was working with inside Gallup and mentioned school districts I was engaging in meaningful conversation. I had no reason to believe her inquisitive nature was anything but an authentic interest in my work. The email described how proud and excited she was about the work I was doing, how she believed it would make a difference in schools and for students, and how I was breaking new ground in our education space to consider new ways of serving my clients.

I felt a rush of adrenaline and pride—until I read her next paragraph. She began to dictate how teams would be organized, who would do the work, and how I was to move forward with projects. She directed the work toward the mediocre White male and "cool group." That "closed mindset" group had gotten to her, and she was planning to protect them. In reality, the "closed mindset" group had always been in her camp as cliques, and power groups were part of the organizational culture. As I was expanding the team, they were growing in fear about their own role, impact, and future. In some cases, I was exposing limitations and titles that did not align with skills and strengths. In her work on shame, Brené Brown talks about how the most shame-inducing emotion at work is the fear of being irrelevant. I was watching that play out in real-time. It wasn't relevance I was seeking to create but rather the ability to provide my school partners with the very best experiences and outcomes our team could deliver. As clients were meeting new partners, they began requesting more of their time, which meant the time of current team members would be minimized. They were in self-preservation mode and growing concerned about their future. And she was going to leverage her power to help them.

Soon a new Education Practice leader was selected, and I was nervous. I had worked with her in the past and knew she lacked the leadership talent to take us where we needed to go. I convinced myself it would be all right and to give her a chance. This was an opportunity to work differently together. I was one of seven consultants who all held a revenue goal. Revenue expectations were established at the team and individual levels. I was expected to contribute fifty percent of the revenue of our team target. No, that was not an error in calculation!

The other six consultants were relatively new and had joined our team within the last year. They still had some growing and learning to do. Company leaders, however, had the expectation that we would continue to grow at their desired percentage rate no matter the experience of our team. I convinced myself that, of course, our new leader would support, protect, and defend me, after all my 50 percent revenue contribution was a key component of her individual goal for the year. So I continued the path I was on and the work I was doing in creating a new direction. I went for it! Throughout the year I was creating new opportunities and on track to meet my target. She could claim my results were due to her leadership. My success was critical to her success. I kept moving forward all the while choosing to keep the peace.

By the middle of that year, the attacks from the "closed mindset" group began to grow. Gossip was rampant. Criticism was everywhere, and I began to feel like a caged animal pacing from corner to corner, not knowing who to trust or how to get out. I became concerned that some of our district partners were not entirely happy with the progress they were making in creating engaged cultures. Most were in their third year or longer with us in doing this work. So I embarked on a nationwide tour to meet with our superintendent and district leader partners. My purpose was to listen and learn from them about what we were doing well and how we could better serve them. In most cases, I did not take members of our team with me as I wanted to be sure they were able to speak honestly and openly.

After several of these interactions, I created a report that would be presented at our next strategy-setting team meeting. I presented the feedback I had gathered from our most trusted and loyal clients and provided suggestions on how better to meet their needs. The way most of the teams at Gallup were structured was that the senior client development consultant—that would be me—would create the best team for every project. That meant sometimes team members would move on and off the project. I would soon find out that this line of thinking was not embraced by our group. Their entitlement to work, position, and title was being questioned and I had the audacity to call it out. I mentioned one of the strategies I would employ in order to better meet client needs and retain them was to change up team members on projects. This action was met with disdain and toxic gossip.

After the meeting, I later discovered team members had the legendary and culture-corrosive "meeting after the meeting" on several occasions. Rather than offering suggestions and ideas during our formal time together, they complained behind my back for doing my job. In future meetings, I watched as team members texted under the table while we were in discussion, jumped on cell phones to talk with absent team members as soon as we adjourned, gossiped in corners about decisions I was making, and played the "favoritism" card with those aligned to company power players.

And in all fairness and with total transparency I engaged in similar behavior. I didn't know how to navigate these toxic waters. I talked with the new leader of our division about who I believed was getting in the way and why. I was hoping she would take it on and protect me. I ran from having really difficult, honest conversations with individuals and turned toward others to have them on my behalf. That way I could stay silent. I thought remaining silent and not directly confronting those who engage in this behavior was keeping the peace. And instead, it was contributing to the battle. It felt so personal. What I know now is that it wasn't personal at all. It was their reaction to the changes, their fear of becoming irrelevant, exposed, and their need to hustle to remain significant. Later that year, I attended an all-company event where I was surprisingly publicly acknowledged as the highest revenue-earning mid-market sales consultant. The contradiction of being talked about and subverted at every turn with being recognized and awarded for performance created an emotional roller coaster I knew I needed to get off.

On July 6, I scheduled two virtual meetings: One with the senior leader of our education practice and one with my direct supervisor. I was going to submit my resignation. I would do so by continuing my toxic practice of "keeping the peace" and showing appreciation for the opportunities the last sixteen years had given me. When I met with the senior leader and told him I was tendering my resignation, he was stunned. He asked, of course, why

I was leaving, but with one caveat. He didn't want to know about any impact my direct supervisor might have had on my decision. That pretty much summed up my reason for leaving. There was no desire to receive honest feedback.

So I stuck to my script. I told him I felt I was no longer able to do my job the way I believed it should be done and how I had done it successfully for the past sixteen years. I thanked him for his support and for all the opportunities to work with school leaders across the country. I offered to stay on until they could find a replacement and that I would work with that person to transition my clients. I had been the lead consultant for so long for many of them. This would be a significant change and I wanted to honor the trust and confidence they had in me and the company. I also suggested I would like to stay on to deliver a presentation for a highly valued client as I had been specifically requested to be the one they wanted for this event. He mentioned he might want me to stay on longer, considering how many clients I had to transfer over. I agreed. My clients' needs were important to me. I also wanted to keep the peace.

Later in the afternoon, I met with our practice leader. By now word had spread like wildfire—that's what happens in a culture where gossip is normalized—and everyone knew I had resigned. She entered the virtual room without looking up, placed her water container, notebook, and pen on the table, and mumbled, "I understand you have something to tell me." I responded and suggested that Gallup was like a small town and gossip traveled quickly and she most likely already knew. She said she did and began to ask some questions. I remember so clearly when she asked what she could have done differently as my supervisor.

I dug deep into my Gallup experience, summoned up some courage, and responded that I was her top sales consultant in the practice, that I was managing fifty percent of the division revenue, and that she should have taken good care of the talent that was under her leadership. I shared that if she had advised the team to be patient I would have sold and created exciting projects they could all work on. I wanted to know she had my back. She never did that. I shared the conversation I had with the senior leader about staying on during the transition and meeting a client's request. She told me she would consider it. And our meeting ended.

That afternoon I received an email from her stating my last day would be in less than two weeks. My time at Gallup would end in ten days. I would do my best to make those transitions in a way the clients deserved and someone else would have to deliver the presentation.

At the conclusion of both meetings, I ran quickly back to my office and immediately sent an email I had already drafted to our entire team explaining my decision, encouraging them to continue the very important work they were doing and to take care of one another. Although the news of my resignation was out, I wanted them to hear directly from me. I spent the next ten days in conversations with district leaders with whom I had built wonderful, trusting relationships over the past sixteen years. I wanted to honor those relationships with a personal call from me informing them of my decision to resign and assuring them they would be in good consulting hands.

But there was one call I was anxious about making. It was to the partners I had worked with for the entire time I was at Gallup, the same ones who'd asked me to present to their district leaders at their summer conference. I didn't want them to feel I had let them down. In fact, this was where I was not going to keep the peace. I was going to let them know I had requested my last day be after their conference as they had been such wonderful partners and loyal clients for such a long time. I wanted them to know I wasn't able to honor their request, and I wanted them to hear it from me. I made that call.

Glenn answered, and I explained the decision I had made and that I would be leaving before his event, that honoring his request wasn't possible, but that I would suggest to their new consultant someone who would do a great job for them. He understood, and I think he intuitively knew there was more to the story.

I also spent time transferring my clients to a new consultant. Talking with the new person about every district and their unique needs and packing my office. As I took every award I had won over the last sixteen years down from my red wooden office shelves, the memories of the projects those awards represented, the team members I worked so closely with to win them, and the impact every glass orb represented came flooding back. Around 11:30 a.m. on my last day, just thirty minutes before my company email would be deactivated and go wherever all old emails go to die, I received a message from the power person, "the legacy," who had kicked off this spiral of events. She thanked me for all my work, acknowledged some of the ways I'd initiated new milestones and expectations for our division, and ended by letting me know, should I need a recommendation, not to hesitate to reach out. I responded with a polite message of gratitude for the opportunities and let her know I would reach out should I need anything. Up to the very last email, I kept the peace. And so ended my career at Gallup.

I was not sure what my second journey would look like. I spent many months with my favorite two guys, Ben & Jerry, and my favorite four-legged canine friend, Sadie. I contemplated the question "What next?" I frantically applied for every job I had a slight interest in taking, interviewed a lot, and turned everything down as nothing inspired me or aligned with my personal mission to make an impact on students and the future of schools. I felt such a great loss and grief. I wholeheartedly wanted to return to the leadership and culture work I had been doing.

One morning, I was having coffee time over the phone with a dear friend. She was asking questions and coaching me around "what's next?" She asked why I had left Gallup, and I told her about their new business model that centered around training and developing organizational experts and individual entrepreneurs as strength coaches. She innocently responded, "Well, why not do that?"

"Why don't you take them up on their model and create a business where you can partner, once again, with school and campus leaders to create thriving leadership practices and cultures?" she asked. "Take your experience, knowledge, and talent for creating strong relationships and create the job you want and love."

Over the past thirty years, I had created a strong personal brand with school and campus leaders across the country, not just from my work at Gallup but in my advocacy work as well. I was a trusted advisor, and many of my former clients appreciated and relied on my expertise, creativity, and advice.

Scott Sonenshein describes in his book *Stretch*, "Stretching is a learned set of attitudes and skills that comes from a simple but powerful shift from wanting more resources to embracing and acting on the possibilities of our resources already at hand." So I stretched. I stretched like I had when my dad had given me a twenty-dollar bill to buy my mom the most beautiful gift I could find. I stretched. I stretched when I desperately wanted more time at home with my two daughters and still wanted to contribute financially to our family. And it worked.

And that takes us back to the beginning of my story. One of the researchers I'd discovered while on my way to my second journey after leaving Gallup was Dr. Brené Brown, a grounded theory researcher at the University of Houston, where she had dedicated decades to discovering the skill sets of wholehearted people and brave, courageous leaders. One of her many *New York Times* best-sellers was recommended to me while I was trying to reckon with my next steps. The book is titled *Rising Strong*, and it isn't hyperbole to say it saved me. It gave me the skill sets I needed to dig my way out of what I perceived to be a failure and rise stronger than I had been before having the experience at Gallup. It allowed me to become unwrapped.

I decided to launch Horner Education Consulting Group and Kelly Peaks Horner LLC. I was excited and scared at the same time. Brené taught me in her writing that emotions are not binary and it is okay to be brave and afraid at the same time. And this, as I have come to know and understand, was the purpose and reason for all the pain and isolation. I would use data and insights from some of my favorite authors, amazing thought leaders, and brilliant researchers such as Brené Brown, Glennon Doyle, Angela Davis, Tasha Eurich, Ibram X. Kendi, Austin Channing Brown, Mikiki Kendall, Resmaa Menakem, Dr. Bettina Love, Michelle P. King, Scott Sonehein, Sonya Renee Taylor, Daniel Pink, and Adam Grant, and so many more. These were great influencers, researchers, writers, and impactors who never came up in my master's degree program or subsequent leadership development experiences but who have a lot to contribute to creating thriving leadership practices and cultures. I would focus most of my efforts on women education leaders. I would provide and create opportunities for them to obtain skill sets not generally taught in traditional leadership development. My new mission is to increase the number of women who lead our schools and who thrive and remain in those positions. I want to move the numbers. I could reach and partner with school and campus leaders in a way that served them best and could possibly break new ground and disrupt how women who lead schools and campuses were developed and supported.

This was my new purpose. And it felt right. It aligned with my values. In 2018, I completed and received my certification as a coach and launched my executive education-coaching practice. Today, I spend a great deal of time diving into the research and data-driven practices that matter and the issues that predict and affect women in education leadership roles. I am disrupting what it means to create a thriving school and campus culture. And I am teaching the skills required for brave, courageous leadership. In 2019, I spent three days with Dr. Brené Brown along with approximately 140 leaders from various organizations, countries, backgrounds, and cultures learning how to teach and deliver the skills she discovered in her research. I became a Dare to Lead™ facilitator. In my work with school leaders that spans from the classroom to the senior district level, I have yet to find anyone who has been trained and developed around these very specific skill sets. It is simply not happening in traditional education leadership programs. I examined the variables around strengths-based development and discovered that just knowing your strengths and receiving feedback on a report is not enough. Creating a culture where authenticity is valued is a key component of the equation.

In 2019, I began working with a forward-thinking and leading-edge provost at a historically Black college. I discovered you can't teach courage-building skills, strengths understanding, and well-being out of context and ignore systemic issues within organizational cultures and lived experiences. This experience initiated my own work on understanding my White privilege, White supremacy, and systemic racism. I continue to do that work and am not at all ready to lead others in this capacity. I might never be ready, as there is so much to learn, unlearn, understand, and radically change. I will, however, be brave in every room I walk into and work to be an ally, accomplice, and a coconspirator for social justice, not just a cheerleader. Understanding our unique strengths is a start in creating an authentic leadership practice, but it is not sufficient. It is not sufficient, especially for women leaders, Black women, and all who have been marginalized by systems and White patriarchal cultures. You can't ask marginalized leaders to simply "lead with your strengths" and you will achieve. It's not that simple. I am, however, learning about the intersection of gender and race and what it is like to, as my good friend and co-author Dr. Kendra Washington-Bass says, live in the "in-between."

Being an entrepreneurial consultant has afforded me experiences and development that would not have typically been presented to me. I connected on social media with an assistant professor from the University of North Carolina, Wilmington, Dr. Kerry Robinson. Kerry develops and supports K-12 education leaders and researches women in leadership, specifically superintendents. She responded to one of my tweets and sent me a direct message inviting me to a further conversation. We met offline and talked about all the possibilities of disrupting the way leadership development is currently presented, especially for women. We shared a common belief that well-being is a significant deterrent and factor for women unable to achieve the highest levels of leadership or even in applying for the positions.

In a July 2021 article written by Vipula Gandhi and Jennifer Robison from Gallup, the authors reveal that five hundred thousand more women than men dropped out of the workforce during the pandemic and that "45% of mothers with school-aged children were not actively working in April 2020, representing 3.5 million women who left active work in a single year." The authors go on to report that "nowhere in the world are female workers less stressed than men."[1] Women's well-being will not be ignored. And something must be done to address it in the workplace.

Kerry told me about a most unique organization and conference experience led and organized by women from around the world, Women Leading Education Across Continents. I found myself at the University of Nottingham in July of 2019 among some of the most talented and brilliant women from all over the world. I listened for three days as they told their stories and presented data on studies they'd conducted on the challenges and hurdles women education leaders encounter at school and on campus. There was one overarching theme, well-being. Of course, well-being in the context of culture and country has nuances and very distinct differences. Women in the United States do not share the exact same well-being struggles as women in Brazil, the Philippines, or Saudi Arabia. Recognizing the uniqueness and the well-being of women globally is a huge issue, and it is defined beyond social and emotional well-being and health.

In most data and research on women's leadership, well-being is a critical factor in recruitment, performance, and retention. I taught about the data and research around well-being in my former job. However, I did not teach it in the context of gender, race, systems, and culture. How can we ask women leaders to express their well-being needs within a patriarchal system, with school boards who don't recognize the discrepancy in expectations they are asking future male versus female principals and superintendents or presidents and provosts who expect the same from all staff and faculty no matter their gender or role?

How can we ask them to be brave and courageous in expressing their needs and at the same time feel safe in retaining their lead-

---

1   Vipula Gandhi and Jennifer Robison, "Wellbeing Stats for Women in the Workplace Show a Need for Change," Gallup.com (Gallup, July 23, 2021).

ership position? There is much work to be done in gender equity, and it's where I want to disrupt the status quo. One-size leadership development does not fit all. And too many programs are based on the experiences of the privileged and centered around the White male at work. So, my new mission? To disrupt education leadership professional development, especially for women, ask courageous questions, pose brave solutions, and engage partners to take on this critical work with me.

So what have I begun to learn and understand? Writer Sue Monk Kidd in her novel *The Dance of the Dissident Daughter* writes this: "There is no place so awake and alive as the edge of becoming. But more than that, birthing the kind of woman who can authentically say, 'My soul is my own,' and then embody it in her life, her spirituality, and her community is worth the risk and hardship." Intentionally and specifically knowing and valuing who I am and how I can contribute is essential and is my becoming. I am becoming unwrapped. It is the core of authenticity—it is a step toward tearing down those self-protection practices like "keeping the peace" we all put up to keep from being seen. And it keeps me from calling upon my con or hustler in order to be worthy of belonging and all that I long for.

Once again, I lean on the words of Glennon Doyle,

Quit waiting to get picked; quit waiting for someone to give you permission; quit waiting for someone to say you are officially qualified and pick yourself.

—FROM *UNTAMED*

I have learned many lessons and worked to undo many social conditionings, behaviors, and practices that harmed my psyche, confidence, and well-being. I have learned never again to wait for someone else's permission and to unleash, "untame," unwrap the lessons, behaviors, thoughts, and conditions that were ingrained in me all my life. I pick me. Every damn time!

I want to share those lessons and experiences with women and particularly with women who lead classrooms, schools, districts, and campuses. Lessons of taking responsibility for our own well-being, understanding what we do best and the value of our strengths, and living with the paradox of competing emotions while pursuing the work we love. I want us to create healthy boundaries and live our truth. I want to courageously call out the system of schooling that was not created by women or for women and work to constructively disrupt it in order to create one where we all belong. I want to recognize and deconstruct our internalized misogyny. I choose women to do this work with. My heartbreaks, triumphs, failures, and successes have led me to you. Together, we will explore more deeply why I'm convinced you're the cornerstone of all that is good in our world and the answer to all that is not.

1. Well-being matters. The well-being of women who are leaders matters a lot. It matters in order for us to show up every day authentically and in all our humanity. It matters in order to live out and remain in our values and productively use our strengths.

2. Vulnerability is everything. It is courage, hope, fear, happiness, love, risk, and fragility. It is our duty to establish spaces for ourselves and other women leaders and create cultures and systems where we can thrive. We will meet the researcher and storyteller Dr. Brené Brown in more detail while on this journey together. She tells us that "there is no change, innovation, and creativity without vulnerability."

3. Gender and Race. Understanding the patriarchal structure that women in leadership have to navigate is critical to creating a thriving leadership environment but doing this absent racial context only perpetuates the divide among women. Women of Color navigate the "in-between" of both gender and race. Their stories must be told and listened to. It is critical to ensure that the space created supports the well-being of all.

4. Disrupt. We must do more than gather. Gathering together as women leaders and telling our stories is important but not enough. Let's disrupt education and leadership professional development. Let's disrupt the systems that prevent women from thriving. And, together, let's figure out how to build them back up so more women are leading schools, districts, and campuses.

I don't propose to know all the answers. And this book does not purport to cover all the issues women face in the workplace. We don't address every issue faced by all marginalized groups within the education community. But it's a start. I do know a few things for sure based on my experience. There needs to be change, and that change will ultimately come from us. Reading a quote by American novelist and nonfiction writer Anne Lamott allowed me to own my story. She said, "You own everything that happened to you. Tell your stories. If people wanted you to write warmly about them, they should have behaved better." That was all the permission I needed. I spent the first year post-Gallup exploring, analyzing, and therapizing over what I should and could have done differently. I did that work. Now let's do this work together.

That's my story. Story is our best data. What lessons have I learned?

1. I was raised and conditioned to keep the peace for others at the expense of my own internal peace. How were you socially conditioned? What have been the patterns of behavior in your life? Write your origin story.

2. Explore how your patterns of socialized behavior show up at work. Have they helped you achieve your goals? How have they been an obstacle?

3. What new words and vocabulary do you need to speak up for yourself and for other women you lead, work and live with? Seek new skills, learnings, and understandings that will allow you to show up as a brave new you.

4. Explore what it means to be an ally, accomplice, and coconspirator.

KENDRA'S ORIGIN STORY
I AM HERE

You've got to learn to leave the table when love's no longer being served.

—Nina Simone

THERE WAS NO "broken" home, no drug-addicted mother, no abject poverty—at least, I did not know I was poor or my home was broken. My life was good. I had a mom who told me she loved me and extended family who had each other's backs. So, why do you want to hear my story? Quite frankly, I am not her. I want to rewrite the narrative about women—Black women. Especially Black women who lead. We are bombarded with images of women wagging fingers, rolling necks, and who are oversexed. We are perceived as weak, too emotional, sole nurturers, and yet, strong enough to bear constant trauma and pain. Images, videos, and music lyrics tout us as whores, bitches, chicken heads, and tricks. I am not her. I am writing this story to proclaim that the images you see are not typical. It is a caricature of thoughts once expressed by our oppressors. I will use my voice to tell my real story and change the narrative. I am here and I want you to see me.

I grew up in a family where the women were the strong ones— the ones in charge, not because they chose to but because they had to. This was clear from the time that I can remember. The tall-in-stature and loud-in-the-mouth women took care of the household, made family decisions, bailed people out who were in trouble, kept the finances in order, and doled out advice even when you thought you didn't need it. As a young girl, I did not understand the advice. The twisted tongue of colloquialisms or family sayings from the South held little meaning to me, but now I see it: "Every shut eye ain't 'sleep. Every goodbye ain't gone, ''How you like dem apples?" and my mom's long-standing family favorite, "A guilty conscience needs no accuser."

I was blessed to know my great-great-grandmother, great-grand-mother, grandmother, and mother. I saw them interact with each other, exchanging life stories at the kitchen table playing cards or cooking family dinners on the weekends—five generations of women, each silently battling and fighting through life to maintain home and family in a world that fought ferociously against them. I am here because of them. The lessons I learned were from watching them navigate life's twists and turns, moments of joy and disap-pointment, loss and blessings, and abundance and sacrifice. These women created a roadmap for how I would be as a Black woman, mother, wife, teacher, and leader.

In 1985, the course of my life was changed by one decision my mother made for our family. She was selected among hundreds of people in New York City, under then-Mayor Ed Koch's initia-tive to provide access to affordable housing to low-income families and to purchase a home in the Bronx. This was an opportunity to have something we would call our own. I heard stories of the large swaths of land that my elders worked and harvested in the South. They spoke of land that their family may have owned and how it was taken from them. They also spoke of the land forgotten by a generation who wanted to erase the memories of the horrors of the South. I could only imagine a place like that since I only knew the cramped apartment in Harlem we shared with various family members and friends. My mind was swirling with excitement. My mother, brother, and I would be moving to a three-bedroom, one-and-a-half-bathroom home with a backyard! I was going to have my own room and my own stuff. A lifestyle I imagined in the television shows I watched as a kid like *The Brady Bunch* and *Diff'rent Strokes*. The home would have a beautiful front yard dotted with flowers, butterflies fluttering, and birds chirping in the morning. There would be a sprawling staircase leading to spacious bedrooms with fancy beds adorned with lush duvet covers and pillows. My room would be pointedly decorated with florals or prints of black-eyed Susans, my favorite summer flower. We would eat dinners together at a well-dressed dining table with decadent desserts. Maybe we would have a dog to round out our new lifestyle. We were going to live the perceived American dream.

I was born and raised in Harlem, the birthplace of the Black renaissance. My mother was eighteen years old when I was born, and two years later welcomed my brother, Bryant. My mom and dad had a brief marriage, and in 1976, my mom moved back in with my grandparents and uncle in a three-bedroom apartment in Harlem. She had already graduated high school and was a college student at the age of sixteen. My mother was overloaded with the responsibilities of raising a family as a single mother, studying and attending college to become a physical therapist, and doing it all while we lived with my grandmother, grandfather, uncle, brother, and a myriad of extended family members and friends who needed a brief place to stay between moves or until they could get on their feet. It was not unusual to wake up in the morning and see someone sleeping on the daybed near our apartment front door and others on the pull-out couch in the living room.

My grandmother, the matriarch of the family, kept law and order. She fed us well in the best way she knew how. I remember her cutting the store-bought liverwurst into thin slices, laying it on top of thick-cut government cheese, and spreading mayonnaise on a hamburger bun. She then quickly broiled it so that the buns were crusted, and the cheese would melt, leaving a slight air pocket on the top. Lunch was served. She was inventive like that, taking the least and making the most. She would say, "You ain't old enough, and you ain't grown enough," when I thought I could give my two cents to any conversation. I learned a lot from her. I watched her every move as she navigated life's challenges. I saw how she tried to take control of a life that seemed to meander out of control. One thing that brought her confidence was her ability to control her household. She ruled the household with a stern look and an occasional heavy hand.

There was an interesting juxtaposition about her. On the one hand, she was a hard woman—decisive, stern, and fearless. And yet, she was gentle and warm. She wanted me to be a lady, giving me tips on how to apply makeup, lecturing me on my posture, and giving me advice on how to stay safe in the streets. She would say, "Kendra, sit up straight. You need to have good posture," "Look at those knees. A lady has clean knees." But when it was time to protect myself, she taught her home-grown dose of self-defense, modeling the keys-between-the-knuckles tactic, or telling me to scream fire at the top of my lungs at the sign of trouble. Sometimes, I annoyed her with my scraped knees, wild hair, and loud voice. At times, I can see her wave the proverbial white flag and resort to telling it to me straight. "Kendra, the world will eat you up and spit you out. You have to be smarter than the next person. Don't let anyone put you down. You are strong. Remember that."

I always knew there was more to her story. I could hear it in the melodies she sang, the days when she would remember what her life could have been—a jazz singer, model, entertainer. She watched endless musicals and sang every showstopper—*West Side Story*'s "America," *Sound of Music*'s "Climb Every Mountain," and *South Pacific*'s "Some Enchanted Evening." All of it drowned in lazy days sipping from her yellow cup filled with tomato juice and gin, sitting on the living room couch, watching *Ryan's Hope*, *All My Children*, *One Life to Live*, and *General Hospital*, in that order. The soaps were her escape into the fantasyland she once dreamed of for herself. Now, she had big dreams for my mother and me. I saw it in her eyes. Those fleeting dreams became her high expectations and hope for her dream deferred.

My mother was driven and an excellent student. She skipped two grades in high school and was the first person in our family to attend college. She worked long hours in her PT rotations and studied in most of her spare time. My mom became a practicing physical therapist in her early twenties, and she was a natural caregiver—always concerned about others' well-being. When the house was full of people drinking, playing cards, or listening to music, my mother would close the door to her bedroom to study or play with me and Bryant to bide the time. I remember her quietly escaping to the bathroom to read, clear her head, or get away from it all. Even though she rarely complained, I saw the tiredness in her eyes. The load of responsibilities weighed heavy on her and as a young woman, this was a lot to bear. My brother and I loved to look out the window of the apartment around 6:00 p.m. to see her pull into the adjacent parking lot, get out of her gray Toyota

Corolla, and wave at us. There were times she would just sit in the car, staring at the windshield, or hanging her head. I knew she was exhausted, but she forged ahead. She cleaned the house, did the shopping, kept the peace, and helped us with our homework. There were days I saw her frustrations—trying to figure out why she seemed to bear the majority of the responsibilities. She would ask my grandmother, "Why don't you ask David to clean up and go shopping? It's not fair."

My Uncle David also lived in the house. He was two years younger than my mother and he got away with murder. He would hang out with friends, eat most of the food in the fridge, and complain about not having anything to eat. He rarely cleaned, and when he did, it was because company was coming. One afternoon, I decided to surprise my mother by baking her a cake in the new Easy Bake oven I had gotten for Christmas. I remember the pride I felt after I mixed the chocolate batter and poured it into the four-inch pan to cook under that hundred-watt bulb in the small tabletop oven. I decorated the cake with a glaze of chocolate icing and multicolored sprinkles. I displayed it properly on the kitchen counter on a dessert plate with a napkin and fork. I was eager to see her face after a long day of work when she walked into the kitchen to enjoy her treat.

The surprise turned to devastation and anger when the cake disappeared. A few sprinkles dotted the place where the cake had been displayed. Uncle David ate it! He ate the whole thing like it was a petit four. My mother was irate. My grandmother chased him to his room with a broom, but he barely apologized for it. There was definitely a difference in the way my grandmother treated my mother and uncle. My grandmother depended on my mother's strength and, in some ways, hoped for a better life for her, for us.

She knew that my mother would be okay on her own—she had to believe so. She saw in my mother what she had hoped to become.

The seeds were planted for how I would make sense of the world and my life in it. The Bronx life was very different from my Harlem upbringing, and my initial perceptions of the American dream. Our house was quiet. The three-bedroom house between 180th and 181st on Prospect Avenue in the Bronx was a little slice of peace. These sixteen houses were nestled between two vacant lots and sat in a valley surrounded by six-story tenement buildings. Working-class Black and Hispanic families lived in these homes, and our presence there was met with a lukewarm reception. We were the "bougie" families who'd moved into their neighborhood, and they let us know it. I never thought of us as middle-class or bougie, but the fact that we owned a home separated us from the others in the neighborhood.

I had just entered high school, at the height of the crack and AIDS epidemic. While our home was quiet, violence, sickness, and death surrounded us like a cloud of thick smoke. The flowers and shrubs planted in the front of the house soon disappeared, leaving gaping holes in the soil. Cars parked in the carport were stripped of tires, hubcaps, and even the side mirrors. Soon after, we installed gates on the windows—main and top floor—gated the carport, and installed a makeshift alarm system to prevent any more plant thieves. One jingle of the bell rigged to the top floor of my mother's bedroom signaled an attempted plant-napping. It was as if we were imprisoning ourselves. I recall one evening when the "alarm" went off. My mother took off down the stairs with a pitchfork in hand. She stumbled across the patch of land where there was now a gaping hole and ran up to the dark figure. She held the pitchfork to the throat of the man who had a shopping cart full of plants he had "accidentally" taken from the neighbors' homes.

"I didn't know it was you, miss," the man whimpered in a shaky voice, arms raised as the pitchfork pointed near his bulging Adam's apple.

"You do not know me! Give me my plants back! If I see you here again, it will be your last time alive." My mom was about it. I guess this was the first time she started to fight for environmental and food justice.

Walking to school was an obstacle course of beggars, crack vials, and addicts. Graffitied memorials of Black and Brown boys flanked the streets like oversized tombstones—a reminder of how my life or that of my brother could be extinguished. I wanted the comforts of what was known, and this new place felt like seeing my death. Each day was a stark reminder of the words my grandmother etched into my brain. I had to change the narrative. I had to be different. I had to be strong.

How could this be? What happened to those fantasized dreams of a home full of promise? This part of the American dream was very different from the images I'd read in books or seen on television shows. The lives of Black and Brown kids were different. Is it more of Langston Hughes's dream deferred? While we were homeowners, our house was small and family dinners were fleeting. My mother continued to work long hours and weekends attending to her home-bound patients to pay for the Catholic education for my brother and me. My mom opted to send my brother and me to Catholic school after she came to eat lunch with me at P.S. 200 in Harlem when I was in kindergarten. Apparently, the kids on the playground during recess were "cussing like longshoremen," and that was the end of my public school experience. She withdrew me from the school immediately and enrolled me at St. Mark the Evangelist School in Harlem from kindergarten through eighth grade and I continued my Catholic school education through high school.

My mother was one of the few physical therapists serving patients in Harlem and the South Bronx. Since she was also one of the very few Black therapists, she was in high demand to serve these same communities. As we navigated the streets of the South Bronx, she navigated the dangerous housing projects and tenements to visit her patients. She risked her life every day, alone, with her smarts, charm, and a fierce fight for the patients in her care. My brother and I took what we learned from our grandmother and cousins and made dinners, cleaned the house, and tried to ease the stress on my mother. We continued to witness her tireless sacrifices, and we tried to lessen any additional stress, especially as we were evolving teens. We also used our street smarts to make friends and gain protection in the hood. We formed a new community.

That same year, I met Jason. His "play cousin," Sean, moved across the street from my house, and during the summers and on some weekends, Jason would hang out with us on the block. We played loud rap music in front of my house, went to the neighborhood carnival, and hung out on the sidewalk snapping on each other and telling "yo' mama" jokes. I did "like" him for about two weeks, and then it was over.

"Like" was the childhood term used to signify that you were dating someone without all of the gushiness of teenage love. You may hold hands or exchange a brief kiss, but that was all. He was the bigheaded boy whose cousin lived across the street. That is what love was like when you were twelve and thirteen. Little did I know how important he would be in my life. But as a young teen, boys were a fleeting interest that was replaced with my other love—basketball.

I needed to busy myself because the war on drugs was killing us. Every week, there was another memorial to mark the short and tragic life of a young Black or Latinx boy. To get away from the terror awaiting us in the streets, I played varsity basketball and was captain of my team. While I was an okay baller, I was a great team-mate and leader. I believe that I was selected captain because of my ability to keep our team focused and remain in control when shit hit the fan. And we had many times and opportunities for the shit to hit the fan. If you played basketball in NYC, you were part of an elite group. Competition and rivalry were fierce on the courts. This is where you grew up. Some of the most decorated men and women who ever played the sport cut their teeth on the courts of the New York City playgrounds, like the Rucker or the Cage.

And this was where legendary coaches were born. Ms. Santos, my coach, exemplified the toughness and tenderness of a New York City b-ball coach. She was hard as nails and yet, had the biggest heart. She was the epitome of a leader. She saw what we could become and never wavered in her expectations for us. And those expectations were high. I can recall playing a game against St. Barn-abas High School, a predominantly White Catholic school in the northern section of the Bronx. There was a clear divide among us—they were White, and we were Black, Brown, and very rough around the edges. They did not hide their disdain for us, and nei-ther did we.

I thought it was simply fierce competition until we came out on the floor and their fans began to call us "niggers," "dykes," and "spics."

You can imagine how the "Black, Brown, and very rough around the edges" girls responded. It took all of my four-foot, ten-inch, 105-pound frame to hold back the anger and hurt of the team. Ms. Santos and I had to pull them back and focus the team on beating them on the court. She gritted her teeth, pointed her finger at us, and said, "Take all of the emotions—hurt, anger, shock—and jam it down their throats on the court." I have seen her angry, but this was different. She wanted us to fight for our dignity.

We ate them up that night! We were like a team possessed. Every fabric of our being was conjured to make a point. We are worth it. It was a significant turning point in our lives. We left with the realization that as young women, we had taken a collective stand. This was one of the first times in my life where I experienced the power of collective sisterhood.

Aquinas High School was an all-girls Catholic school in the Bronx. It was awarded the National School of Excellence and one of the top-rated all-girls high schools by the Archdiocese of New York. Like my mother, I was a hardworking student and excelled in all of my classes. I was in the National Honor Society, Spanish Honor Society, the varsity basketball captain, and service award recipient. I was an unofficial advocate for my classmates and always spoke up when I thought there were inequities among us. I was also the friend who would tell you if you did not do right and was open to feedback to be better.

There are so many parallels to how I saw my mother work, a driven advocate who excelled in school, found a sisterhood in sports—she played college basketball and league softball—and focused on being a leader among her family and peers. I started working when I was fourteen years old, proctoring New York City civil service exams at the high school. While my mother was working long shifts attending to patients and putting in extra hours on the weekends to pay for our Catholic school tuition, I wanted to help. I remember those days my mother paused in her car before heading upstairs to our apartment to give us energy. I wanted to give what she was giving to me.

When I received my first paycheck, I bought groceries and paid for my school supplies and other odds and ends that were needed. These were silent gestures, a contract my mother and I had. There was never a request for help, but an understanding that you did it because it was the right thing to do. There is an unspoken agreement that if anyone needs something, you just give. We still operate like this today. You should see us today at the grocery store fighting to see who can place the credit card in the reader before the other.

A strong work ethic coupled with the expectation that you help your fellow brother or sister is how I live my life now. All of what I saw in my female elders and the new sisterhood I formed at Aquinas reinforced my idea of the strength and leadership in women. I was surrounded, embraced, and encouraged by strong women. I longed to make them proud, and stand strong on their shoulders. This was an education that you cannot get in a school, but the significant life lessons that go far beyond the classroom walls. What if we can embed these lessons within the classroom? Ms. Santos did it, and so many others in my educational life—Ms. Alexander, Mr. Edwards, Ms. Jefferson, and Ms. Esthridge—taught the lessons beyond the lesson. These are the lessons that sustain. Those of resilience, persistence, humbleness, and grit continued to be etched into my mind.

My mother always wanted my brother and me to "spread our wings." She never put limits on what we aspired to be, and she encouraged us to live out our dreams. I knew I wanted to go away to school. With New York continuing to battle gang violence, the crack epidemic, and the virus, I wanted to escape, to be in a different environment where I thought I could breathe and concentrate. My naivety and need for an escape led me to the University of Notre Dame in 1990.

South Bend, Indiana was a world of difference from Prospect Avenue in the Bronx. I figured I was smart enough, driven enough, and responsible enough to make it through. What a rude awakening! The only thing that the South Bronx and South Bend had in common was the word *South*. I was now thrust into unknown territory with people and experiences that were dissimilar to mine.

"How did you get here?"

"Are you on a sports scholarship?"

"Were you part of affirmative action?"

"You were part of the quota for Blacks."

At first, I brushed this off as ignorance and their own lack of experience with interacting with Black people. But when the threats became more overt and the harassing phone messages were amplified, it became too much to bear. Messages were being left on my voicemail: "You monkey! Go back to Africa! Niggers don't belong here. You were nothing but a worthless slave. That is why your name is Washington! Your family was only good enough to be Washington's whores."

I remember going to campus police with the notes and recording and leaving the offices with no answers or help. They shrugged their shoulders or asked if I'd offended someone in my dorm or class. Oh, blame me for the treatment. Really? I remember talking to professors who felt their hands were tied. I also tried to find out how campus administration could help only to find out that there was no racial harassment policy in place. I remember asking my RA for help and needing to share what was going on. They thought I was making it a "big deal." I even went to those who I thought could help—the football players. Yeah, they have influence and could help. Dead end.

"I cannot get involved."

"My scholarship."

"What did you do to piss someone off?"

So, now I am a victim twice. Unbelievable! I worked hard and deserved to be there, but I was terrified and alone. How could I navigate the war that was occurring in my South Bronx neighborhood but struggle in this South Bend community? Thirteen hours from home and getting in a car and leaving campus was not a viable option. I remember calling my mother and stating that when I came for Christmas, I was not going to go back.

Her words and the tone in her voice still resonate today. As she gritted her teeth, she said, "You will not let them beat you. You deserve to be there. Don't let anyone take that away from you. You are going to stay there, and you will show them by getting that degree." Then she went on a rant about how she was calling Jesse Jackson and Al Sharpton and will be shutting down the university.

That is when I had to pump the breaks. I got it! All of the lessons rushed back. This was what I was prepared for—to fight. My grandmother, mom, and teachers planted the seed of resilience that I needed to push back, stand my ground, and show that I am worth it even if others did not think I was. So I put words to action, joined three student groups, was a member of a student-created activist group, Students United for Respect (SUFR), held sit-ins at the administration building, spoke up in classes against racists and misogynistic comments, and pushed back on my advisor who wanted to place me in a class that statistically could not be possible—an all-Black literature class. Really?

The university did not have a racial or sexual harassment policy that could protect students from these aggressions. And the community of Black students was so small that our voices seemed to be drowned out by others who thought we were annoying complainers who just needed to adjust to the "way of life" on campus. How did we get here? These young students seemed to be holding on to generations of ideas that did not seem to fit the times. So, I continued to speak, protest, push back and fight for ways to improve the conditions for Black students at the university. This meant creating a network of peers to keep us safe as we navigated racist and misogynistic spaces.

At Notre Dame, I studied film and television and loved the art of storytelling and the visual depiction of lived experiences. I was intrigued by the cinematography of classic works, the plot twists and turns, and occasionally surprising endings. I also noticed how these stories seemed to depict partial truths or untruths. There was always a second story or backstory that if you looked closely, you could miss or subliminally absorb, particularly stories about women, Black, Latinx, and Indigenous people. I wanted to tell the backstories but was not prepared to continue this journey in graduate school. The cost was prohibitive. I did not expect my mother to help me, and I did not ask.

I thought of another way to tell the story, to help kids like me and the ones that I met who just did not have the story right. I pivoted and applied to this little-known program at the time, Teach for America (TFA). I can remember seeing the flyer on a posterboard in the student center. I tore the little slip of paper and contacted the number for an application. I decided that I could change the narrative by melding the minds of children. I was fortunate that, after graduating from Notre Dame and getting accepted to TFA, I was placed in New York City. In fact, I was hired at an elementary school in the neighborhood near my high school in the Bronx.

It was an interesting circle—the area I wanted to initially escape, I was brought back. Everything happened for a reason. It was meant to be. When I returned to New York, Jason and I reconnected, and the once fleeting teenage crush turned into more serious feelings. We fell in love as if we always knew we would be together. While it was weird that I would be marrying the "bighead boy from across the street," we had stayed friends from the time we met in 1985. We talked often, went to the movies, and hung out at family gatherings. I did not know then how our friendship would blossom into our relationship today, but he was always there. My relationship and love for him would challenge and change the way that I navigate life as a woman, wife, parent, and leader.

I worked as an elementary and middle school teacher in the West Farms section of the Bronx for nine years. I remember my first day as a fourth-grade teacher. It was hot, and the streets were filled with parents walking their children to school with oversized book bags. They were holding their hands in anticipation of a great year. Kids either clenched their mothers' hands with the excitement of meeting new friends or the fear of leaving mommy. We met our students on the asphalt parking lot/playground where yellow-painted markers were placed for each grade level and classroom.

My classroom number was 416. I was expecting 36 students in my class and had to come up with an ingenious way to make sure that I had desks and materials for all students. It required some rotating carpet squares, shared supply bins, and lots of movement between desks. While holding up my makeshift sign with the room number and my name, a mother came up to me and asked if I was the teacher. I excitedly told her, "yes," and then she pushed her son toward me and said, "Good luck with my son."

Gilberto gave that grin that only new teachers understand. He was going to be trouble, or so I thought.

I loved my students. They were so hard and yet yearned for hope. They wanted what all kids want—to be cared for, loved, and to have someone cheering for them. I saw their potential and I also saw the heavy burdens they bore as nine-year-olds. Nine-year-olds bearing the weight of poverty, dysfunction, abuse, violence, and loneliness, and yet, they were hopeful and eager every day to start anew. They were yearning for something better, even if they weren't sure what better was. The responsibility and power I had in my hands to help them reach "better" were enormous. On the one hand, I understood their plights, and in other ways, I was different from them.

I did what I could to teach them about life through the life lessons taught to me—formal and informal. I managed my classroom like each student was my family. I had very high expectations in my classroom and showed empathy when necessary. Excuses were not necessarily accepted, and my students seemed to blossom. I took a page from Mrs. Santos' school of tough love. I did not realize how much I would love teaching, but it was the right career decision. It brought me joy every day when I was able to see my students go from being uncertain and apprehensive about learning, to eager and excited about learning something new or seeing things from a different perspective.

I took my students on field trips often and infused history and the arts within the lessons. I felt my students needed to see positive images of themselves and learn about ways to be successful and navigate a world so much wider than our neighborhoods. I saw my students as a collection of excited, funny, ingenious kids with old souls. It was as if they had lived here before. They knew things that I did not know as a child. They understood the rules of the hood and were able to navigate it better than I did, and they learned how to survive even through some unimaginable circumstances. I wanted them to see that their minds were needed in the world and that they could shift from endless survival tactics to thriving. How could I harness that energy and that fever throughout life? My experiences with them affirmed my readiness to start a family.

Jason and I had been married four years when we had Julian. He was such a good baby. He always smiled and had a voracious appetite. He was smart and seemed to move through the world at lightning speed. He was our world, and after several attempts at having children, he was God's blessing for us. We thought that he would be it, and we were so happy to have been blessed to have him. But children can complicate life. Everything revolved around Julian from our sleep and work schedules, downtime, and intimacy. Every thought in my mind started with Julian. At one point, Jason had to grab me by the arm to prevent me from checking on him at night when he cried. Call it first-time parent anxiety or my fear that something would happen to him. I was keenly aware of the world he would have to navigate as a Black boy and man. I feared he could one day be part of the parade of painted murals in the South Bronx with flowers and stuffed animals laying on the gravel as a memorial for his young life. Julian became the center of my life.

I recall one day in the summer of 2001 when my friend, Yvelisse, and I took our children to Jones Beach. It was Julian's first time in the sand and at the ocean. He was playing with Yvelisse's two children when she said to me "You're pregnant."

"What are you talking about?" I looked at her with bewilderment.

"You're pregnant. I can tell." I sucked my teeth.

There were no indications that I was pregnant. I had not missed my period, and Jason and I were so tired that intimacy was on hold. With the other failed attempts before Julian, there was a very slim chance that I could be pregnant. I dismissed her claim as friendly mommy banter. Then, in July, I missed my period. Holy shit! After two pregnancy tests and a doctor's visit, I was indeed pregnant. Jason and I were numb. It was a surprise, and I had a hard time believing it. We were barely making it with one child, but two? I crossed my fingers, prayed, and hoped we could be just as attentive to two as with one.

And then time stopped. On Tuesday, September 11, 2001, life for our family changed. I remember how picturesque the day was. It was warm and the sky was a beautiful crayon sky blue. I had dropped Julian off at the daycare center in Teaneck, New Jersey, and headed to work in the Bronx. I was feeling okay with minimal morning sickness. Traffic was surprisingly light, but people may have been enjoying a long holiday weekend. We had taken a family trip to Six Flags and Julian enjoyed his first major amusement park adventure. I remember Jason and my brother, Bryant, daring to ride the human slingshot and them both saying, "You only live once."

I arrived at school early so that I could make it up the five flights of stairs to my classroom. Community School 6 is a massive building that sits on top of a hill on Tremont Avenue in the Bronx. It was once a medical facility at the turn of the 20th century, and it is deemed a historic site. The views of the city from the top floor are spectacular. That was an added benefit of having a classroom on the upper floor. You had a wonderful view of the New York City skyline, and with the sky so clear, you could see the Empire State Building, Chrysler Building, and the World Trade Center. I had just finished teaching the first lesson on suspense, using the classic movie and short story *The Most Dangerous Game* when I heard a commotion in the hallway. My teammate and friend, Yvelisse, explained that a plane had hit one of the Twin Towers.

I remember going over to her room to look out of her window to see. One of the safety precautions in the building is that the windows started about five feet from the floor, so you had to stand on a chair to see out. I recall barely looking out of the window to see smoke coming from the North Tower. I thought, *What a tragic accident!* LaGuardia airport was not too far from Manhattan and on takeoffs and landings, the flights circled high above the city giving you a picturesque view of the skyline.

Something prompted me to ask Yvelisse if she could call Jason to check on him as I was preparing for my next class. I wrote his number on the chalkboard and left to teach my language arts lesson. There was an uneasiness that I could not shake. There was something off. I felt it in the pit of my stomach. I chalked it up to morning sickness and welcomed my class. They were a bit distracted, but we dove into the reading, and I tried my best to act out the scenes, using a myriad of voices for each character.

Again, something was off. I was usually on my game, but I was unnerved by the image of the smoke coming from the Twin Towers. After I dismissed my class, I went back to Yvelisse's classroom to get a status update on the "accident." I tried to enter her classroom, but the door was locked. The students were huddled near the window with solemn looks on their faces. It was as if they saw me but saw through me. I knocked on the door again, but no one moved. Yvelisse was standing motionless, and her students were silent. I knocked a third time. This time I was yelling for someone to open the door.

One student walked timidly toward the door. "What is going on? Why didn't you open the door? What happened?"

One student answered in the best way he knew how. "They are no more."

I stopped for a minute trying to comprehend what he was saying. "What do you mean they are no more? Move out of the way. Let me see." I stood on the chair and saw what would have been a beautiful sparkling metallic skyline, now a large plume of smoke as if the city was being choked. The towers were no longer visible. It seemed like time stopped. I just stared out hoping that my eyes would focus and the towers would appear. That never happened.

I stepped down off the chair and walked backward almost in slow motion to the door. Panic filled my body, and I felt my body go weak. I ran downstairs to my principal's office. I could barely get a word out when he stated that my mother had called and said she was on her way to pick me up.

"Pick me up? Oh my God, Jason is dead." I felt lightheaded and weak in the knees. I am a widow with a one-year-old and one on the way. My principal sat me down and gave me a drink of water. Almost everything after that was a blur. I do not even remember how I got to my mom's house, but I was there looking at the television seeing the replay of the planes hitting the towers and people running for their lives as smoke and debris chased them through the financial district.

At the time, Jason was a bank examiner for the Federal Reserve Bank of New York, and he often met his college friend, Kenney Caldwell, for breakfast at a cafe in 1 World Trade Center Plaza. This day, schedules did not allow them to meet, so Jason had gone directly to his office. My worry was amplified when I could not reach him. His phone was either busy or went directly to voicemail. I kept looking at the TV to see if I could see him among the crowds of people running or walking along the East River. Daybreak turned to night so quickly.

While on one hand time seemed to stop, time also sped through the day. The stories of people looking for loved ones are repeated like a recurring nightmare. Would I join them with my pleas for my husband's whereabouts? All of the worries about Julian changed to the image of the mural or memorial of Jason as a victim of a terrorist attack. How will I raise my children? How would I get through this?

My stomach turned, and the air became thin. It had to be about 7:15 p.m. when I was awakened by screams of "He's here!" My mother's neighbor Cheryl yelled," He's here!" The flood of emotions ran through my veins like hot and cold water at the same time. My mother and I ran and collapsed into Jason's arms as we fell to the concrete ground thanking God for sparing his life. He was covered with dust, exhausted, and hollow in his eyes. This day forever changed our lives and our marriage.

After September 11, I really wanted to hold on tighter to my family and find a sense of normalcy and stability. Jason was ready for anything. He was always an adventurous person and now he was jumping headfirst into numerous ventures. I saw him hurting and trying to capture every moment of life. I was trying to slow life down and savor the moments of quiet.

In 2004, Jason quit his job at the Federal Reserve and started a new venture eventually opening up an Edible Arrangements in the spring of 2005, and a few months earlier, I became a middle school principal in Harlem. I was one of the youngest principals in the district and the city. I went from being a middle school teacher in the Bronx to an interim middle school principal in Harlem in one weekend. I felt ready because I had the passion, knowledge of curriculum development, and student engagement. It was a whirlwind moment.

Julian and Justice were four and two years old. Our life was in a constant state of movement. We leaned on family and friends to help us navigate childcare, work, social life, and rest. Edible Arrangements became a family and friends' business. My mother, cousins, and family friends created the arrangements, ordered food, worked the counters and phones, and made deliveries. I was working long hours as a new principal and, at times, brought the kids to school with me on Saturdays to help set up enrichment classes.

Where was the lesson on "balance" in my principal preparation program? No one really told me how much my life would change as a school principal. I learned how to balance the budget, monitor curriculum, and identify legal aspects of the work, but no one shared the social stressors, personal and professional imbalance, and the sacrifices that may pit work against family life.

At work, I was trying my best to be the leader the school needed. On the one hand, my district superintendent expected specific "fixes," and the teachers, students, and parents needed and wanted something else. There was a constant flux of competing priorities, and I did not have many people to share my struggles with.

My school was located on the east side of Harlem at the intersection of the South Bronx and Spanish Harlem. A bridge to the South Bronx and Queens provided a gateway of commuters who whizzed past our school daily. My school sat on the top floor of a shared building with two other schools, an elementary school on the second and third floor, and a special education school on the first floor. Every day, I saw the untapped potential of my students. They were so smart and they were trapped by circumstances. I saw the inner battles they were having just as I had had as a student. They were me in more ways than they knew.

But there were constant battles of beliefs and ideas about supporting Black children and their development, especially in middle school. I was not prepared for this battle, a battle with my people. I naively thought that we would have a common passion, fever, or support for the education of our kids. I was wrong! The infighting among parents and the factions formed surprised me. I did not understand why we were fighting ourselves, and then it hit me. History taught us that this was the way that we continue to oppress ourselves. Wow! I was watching this in real-time, and I was in the middle, trying as a novice to navigate this.

The students were brilliant, and I saw it, but they seemed to be embarrassed by being seen as "smart." It was as if this label was something to avoid. I recall talking with a student who purposefully threw away his homework after the teacher praised his work as a model for how to complete the assignment. I was confused as to why he would ball up his exemplary work and throw it in the classroom trash can. He stated that his friends would make fun of him. He would rather save face than show his brilliance.

I wish that I could say that battle was only the system, but it ran deep. It was the impact of the system and the internalization of that system's oppression. Now, where was this taught in "principal school"? Every day, I came to work and fought hard for my teach-ers, staff, and students to see that they were brilliant. At times, that meant tough love, hard decisions, and at times, disagreements with teachers and parents who wanted me to "let up" or push harder.

In the meantime, the stress was getting to us. We were begin-ning to run in circles in the rat race. We had to do something different. I thought that we should sell the store and that Jason could find another job in finance, but he wanted to sell our home and move the family to Texas. I knew that New York City was choking the life out of him. The city reminded him of the pain and loss he'd experienced. He needed a change of pace.

Jason's brother convinced him that homes were less expensive and that he could find work easily. We visited Lewisville, Texas, and the homes were beautiful, but my spirit stirred. I could not see us there. Jason was anxious. We needed to make a family change, or I was going to lose him. After getting back from Texas, we had a conversation with my cousins who visited from Georgia, and they convinced us to tour Gwinnett County, Georgia. Jason jumped at the chance, and after touring and house hunting in one weekend, we put a deposit on a house and put our house in New Jersey on the market.

In the fall of 2006, we sold our home and moved in with my mother until our home in Georgia was built. At the time, we did not plan how we would work, but we needed to make a move. Now, I did not want to leave, and it was an internal struggle to hold on to living in NYC and New Jersey, closest to my immediate family, but Jason was searching for newness and the ability to get from being underwater.

Now, don't get me wrong. I did not happily go to Georgia. On the outside, I kept up appearances, but on the inside, I was angry. I was just beginning my career in educational leadership and poof; it was put on pause. This seemed like a typical married female story. Support your man and put your dreams on hold for now. This was the pain my grandmother bore. This was going against the dreams she had for me. I wondered about my compromise. Was I supposed to feel this way? Guilt swelled within me. I loved Jason, and I would do anything to support him, especially as he was navigating his trauma. But I also wondered if this was part of the perpetual female compromise. So, I trusted him. It was as if he was sensing something.

We moved to Lawrenceville, Georgia, in 2007, just before the housing and job market crashed. We did this right on time. I have to believe it was divine intervention. This move put in motion the next journey of my life, the challenges that I would endure, and the awakening I was seeking for myself. I continued working as a principal to finish out my school year before heading to Georgia permanently. I did not initially have a job in Georgia but became a real estate agent to learn about the school system and neighborhoods in the county. This also allowed me to break away and learn something new.

I was very good at buying and selling because I used some unconventional ways to gain clients—advertising on my car, attending open houses to look for clients, knocking on doors, posting flyers on doorknobs, and hosting first-look open houses. I hustled. I really enjoyed real estate, and it allowed me to exercise my knowledge, leadership, and communication skills.

This also helped me to understand the landscape of Georgia, a place I only knew from the stories of the segregated Deep South, cotton, and peanut farmers, and the history of red-stained soil, the blood, and the tears of my ancestors. People were southern polite with "yes ma'ams" and "sirs" as they addressed you, but the Confederate statues still stood tall in town squares, and the Confederate flag waved at the capitol building, casting a looming reminder of "your place."

Because of the connections, I continued to have with TFA, Heather Anichini, the then regional director, contacted me about a potential opportunity with Gwinnett County Public Schools as the assistant director of the Quality-Plus Leader Academy. It was an opportunity to help support a newly launched principal academy within the district. The executive director was looking for someone who had experience outside of the district, led in an urban school district, and can provide innovative ideas for supporting twenty-first-century leaders. The opportunity piqued my interest, and selfishly, it was an opportunity to learn more about leadership.

I really enjoyed meeting Dr. Glenn Pethel and Ms. Linda Daniels. Dr. Pethel was the consummate southern gentleman who was sincerely interested in diversifying the leadership development department. He was open to discussing the future of leadership in Gwinnett and thought someone like me was the future. I was sold! Sold on the ideas of an open learning environment and an opportunity to build a diverse pipeline that would represent the changing student population. This felt like personal and professional redemption, and an opportunity to relearn and redo school leadership

Ms. Daniels was the epitome of a southern lady. She taught me the "rules of engagement," especially as a northerner. She guided how I would navigate in this primarily southern, White male world and hinted at particular cues for how I should talk and act. Her guidance helped to smooth the transition in ways that kept me from "coming on too strong." It was a defining lesson in survival.

Dr. Pethel always indulged me in the story behind the story. He offered his opinions and sought mine often. I was not sure if some of his questions were rhetorical or if he was testing me to see what I believed or what decisions I would make if I were in certain situations.

Mrs. Daniels always asked the "other question" to get to the "real" answer. She had a charming way of doing it, soft, gentle, and with a smile. It would not be until much later that you realized that she got you to answer a question you did not want to share. She had a way of pulling it out of you.

It was turning out to be a learning environment, and I really enjoyed my new role. I was excited to start a new career and life in Georgia. It was the welcome change that I needed to reignite my passion for helping students and beginning a new life with my family.

Then, in October 2008, our world was rocked again. Jason was laid off from his nearly one-year-old job working for Quiznos. This started a five-year road to recovery and discovery for our family and marriage. The promise of a new life, a new start for our family was tested with the millions of others who were now in the midst of the most devastating financial crisis in modern times. Stocks plummeted, companies were laying off workers to stay afloat, and a once-booming housing market was flooded with foreclosures. I thought that this was just a small bump in the road, but Jason could not find a job. The job market was bleak, and the connections we'd made in Georgia were still too new. Jason's demeanor fluctuated from depression to creativity. Just when a thought or opportunity seemed to come to fruition, he was dealt devastating blows. "Sorry, we decided to not hire," or "Great idea, but we decided to go in a different direction."

You never know how this changes a man until you see it unfold right before your eyes. He tried to hide his frustration, but I saw the light in him dim each day. I was becoming increasingly frustrated because I felt the weight on my shoulders to keep us together. This went on like a vicious cycle of personal, professional teasing. One day, there was hope, and the next day, there was a letdown.

Julian and Justice were eight and six at the time and did not seem to have a care in the world. They loved having dad home, and he relished the time with them. I tried to remain calm and resorted to what I had been taught by the women in my family—take care and take control. I went into breadwinner mode, and Jason became the caregiver to Julian and Justice. Needless to say, this was fine in the beginning but as the months turned to a year and then two, the stress got to us. We did our best to hide it from the kids and each other. Jason dabbled in a few opportunities from online teaching to selling cars at a local dealership. While there was nothing steady for a few years, he was able to get the kids on the school bus, take them to karate, have lunch with them at school, check homework, and occasionally make dinner that was semi-tasty.

At my job, I was promoted to director and then received recognition for acquiring and maintaining two major grants that really helped our department to minimize the effects of the economic downturn. Dr. Pethel encouraged me to continue with my education and get my doctorate. He always said that I had a bright future in the district and that the future did not look like, nor should it, look like him.

I followed his guidance and launched into a doctoral program in 2010. I had the full support of my family especially when I promised that I would be finished in three years. And I fulfilled that promise and graduated with a doctorate in educational leadership from Mercer University but not without turbulence and near-marriage-ending consequences. I set a schedule: classes on Mondays and Tuesday nights, writing after work until 7:00 p.m., and then writing on Sundays. I really cranked it out.

What I did not realize was that Jason and the kids starved for my attention. In fact, I was so focused that I dismissed them to live up to my promise. It was as if I went away in plain sight. Our marriage became a partnership, intimacy was intermittent, if any at all, and the kids always saw me "writing." It all came to a head when Jason came into the spare bedroom, which I had converted to an office, and asked me pointedly, "Are you seeing someone?"

I was taken aback. Was he really accusing me? I think I laughed and said, "Yes, and his name is PhD." When he looked back at me without smiling, I realized he was not kidding. He was hurt. I hurt him and turned my promise into a mad woman's crusade to complete my dissertation at the expense of my family. How did I miss the cues? Where did I go wrong? For the first time, I realized the lessons instilled in me at an early age about being strong and taking control did not necessarily fit into this life. It was not needed the way my mother or grandmother needed to behave. I was in partnership with someone and he was keeping his bargain—for better or worse and I was making things worse.

This was an awakening and the first time that I really had to wrestle with the lessons learned and taught to me by the women I greatly admired. I never learned how to partner, especially with a man. At this point, we had been married for seventeen years, and I had to learn to be a wife—in the middle of an economic crisis, a dissertation, and marriage under stress. We stumbled through, scheduling dates, and agreeing that it would get better once I graduated. And it did for a while. The freed-up time allowed us to reconnect and enjoy each other's company. The boys were entering middle school, and they needed our attention more as they explored being teens and tweenagers.

At work, I was thriving. The effort I put in was lauded as high levels of work ethic and dedication. I received many accolades for a job well done. On the inside, my spirit was stirring. How can I be applauded for commitment and dedication at work and struggle and be dismissive at home? These two parallel universes were beginning to collide. My work was expanding, and I collaborated on two major grant projects that had me expand my circle of influence and professional colleagues. As I gained greater exposure, I began to sense something very different happening within the office. Information was still being shared but at a distance. I had to ask permission to attend or participate in meetings when I'd never had to before. By this time, Mrs. Daniels was "asked" to retire, and our office onboarded three new directors. While the reorganization of the office seemed like a logical move, the dynamics changed especially now that the office was all female except the boss, Dr. Pethel.

At first, I was happy to have a new sisterhood. It reminded me of the Aquinas High School teammates. We would be of one accord and tackle the work with a strong bond. But that did not happen. The person I leaned on to help me navigate these waters was gone. What transpired was rivalry, distrust, and competition for projects and attention. For the next few years, we spent time positioning ourselves like one of Charlie's Angels. The stereotypical bickering and backstabbing that I only saw from a distance or watched on *The Real Housewives of Atlanta* were happening here. I became insecure and doubted whether I was good enough. I tried to anticipate my colleagues' moves and protect myself from being run over by what I perceived as a threat to my career. I would come to work early so that I could have some conversations with Dr. Pethel—to gauge what he was thinking. I wanted to be the first to know what his next moves would be. I would stay late to reflect on what I was doing right and wrong and then start this routine over the next day.

My confidence began to wane. Maybe my time in this school district was coming to an end. I went into a depression that was unrecognizable to most people and even myself. I just constantly dissected myself like a specimen under a microscope. I had done everything "right." I learned the rules of engagement and, for the most part, abided by them. I went back to school and received my doctorate, toned down my dress—suits and dresses with heels and, at times, pantyhose. I listened more than I typically talked, especially in meetings with the members of the superintendent's cabinet. At the moment, I was losing myself—losing what made me happy and kept me driven to be my very best. I was now in competition with my female peers. It was not collaboration or support. It was a shot to be on top of a very narrow field and we were tearing each other apart. I played an active role in this melee—choosing jealousy and envy over support and uplifting.

As I reflect on this moment in time, I realize how the opportunities for advancement for women and BIPOC leaders were slim, causing steep competition—a competition to be the first, the only, or the yearning to finally have a seat at the table. For five years, I played this game, participated in this dangerous dance, and had no direction as to how to manage these feelings and experiences. I felt that I was navigating the area of "the in-between," experiencing the constant push and pull to live up to my internal expectations as a Black woman and meet the expectations that my peers, colleagues, and society at large have for me.

This is exhausting! It is like wearing many masks and changing them multiple times within a day, hour, and in some cases within minutes. It was maddening and had a deep effect on my well-being. I kept up appearances and hid my struggles from my friends, families, and peers, but my spirit light was dimming.

At home, another battle waged. I tried to find myself in my marriage, reinserting my alpha female into our relationship. You can only imagine how that went. My personal and professional life was spinning out of control, and I masked it. I buried my anxiety, my surrender, and my feelings deep inside. Keeping up appearances was paramount. As a leader, mom, wife, friend, and coworker, everyone was looking at me. I had to keep it together. This did not last long.

I don't know what happened. A change in our department dynamics, my resolve that my life would continue this way, or a move to a new neighborhood, but I came to the realization that I would not continue to live this way. I continued to hear my mother's voice say, "You will not give up. You are strong." I heard my husband say, "We are partners. Let me help you. Talk to me." I finally broke down and grew up. I found solace in friends. I leaned on them, something that I had not done before. Their daily words of advice or silence helped me rumble. I began to regain my joy despite what was happening around me and I began to learn what I could control. So, how did I get here? This space is where I am once again struggling to find my voice, struggling to be me.

In the spring of 2019, Dr. Pethel announced that he was officially retiring. I was ready! I had done all the preparation I was told I needed. I had "served" my time, gained high levels of confidence with my colleagues, and had a wide range of connections with my education colleagues across the nation. Dr. Pethel and I had candid conversations before he left and reconciled a lot of hurt and pain between each other. He was on my side, an advocate. I think what made him respect me more was the fact that I was resilient. I did not appear to be rattled by what he saw as challenges. He respected my fight. So, when it was time to interview for his replacement, he coached me and set me up for success.

I felt that I had proven my commitment to the organization and that I could sustain the great things that were created and accelerate the department in new and innovative ways. I thought the sacrifices were worth it. And then it happened! The job was given to someone else, a White male high school principal who was a graduate of our aspiring-principal program and my former coachee. Boom!

You see, I have seen this happen to other women and women of color in leadership. I coached them as they recovered from the disappointment and even helped them to reflect on what could have been their DNA on the issue. Maybe they did not have their ducks in a row or did not have some of the prerequisite qualifications that made them the best contender. But here I am, walking in their shoes. I followed the steps! I navigated the "in-between." What more could I have done? And as a consolation prize, I was promoted to executive director and told to help my new boss transition to the role.

Okay, now what? Where do I go from here? How do I reconcile this? How is my leadership going to show in this space? If I had the opportunity to tell the little girl from Harlem and the South Bronx what life would be like in forty years for her, what would I say?

I would say—lean into your friends and family. Do not bury your feelings, depression, and doubts. Let them remain on the surface. The idea of the "strong Black woman" is both empowering and destructive. And the idea of the "strong Black woman leader" is more complicated. People were looking at me and waiting to see my next move. I owe it to myself to sit in my vulnerability and wrestle openly with my new journey. I have concluded that the only one I can change and empower is me. I am enough, and from now on, I choose me!

So here I am. See me. I am opening my personal, professional book to you. I will no longer be used as a pawn for my talents to be robbed and cast aside when I am no longer needed. I am not part of "the plan" and never was. I realize that now. I have the scars to prove it. What lessons have I learned?

1. Begin to work on you, first. Discover who you really are. This may mean going into physical, mental, and emotional rehab.

2. Build a strong, positive coalition of women and people of color. The sisterhood bond can help you show up as an empowerer versus a destroyer.

3. Share tools and strategies with each other so that you can be seen and respected. And if you cannot pull up a seat at the table, then learn to build your own.

4. Lean on our partners (men) to help us. We need them and they need us. The partnership helps to develop healthy relationships needed for allyship and coconspiritorship.

5. Don't compromise who you are. Your well-being depends on it. Continue to refine yourself and be careful of the layers of masks you may be tempted to wear.

6. Listen to your elders but know that they could be wrong. Our elders were wise and their lessons may transcend generations. We also know that their lessons could be time-bound. Seek their guidance and tell them the unscripted truth. This will help them understand the context needed to support your thinking and next moves.

7. Be a teacher. Be a teacher of leaders. Let people know your story and use your experiences to open space for others to help us move from surviving to thriving.

I am here because I have a story to tell. I have lessons to share. I have tools you can use. I want to create a space where we can tell the unscripted truth of the life of women in educational leadership and the contexts that perpetuate misogyny and dismantle the structure to simply keep us afloat, barely keeping our head above water. We want to do more than survive. We want to thrive. I do not purport to know the answers but together, we climb, design our table, take a seat, and get to work!

WELL-BEING MATTERS: MOVING THE NUMBERS

The only way to get what you really want is to let go of what you don't want.

—Iyanla Vanzant

IN JULY OF 2019, I had the extraordinary experience of attending the Seventh International Women Leading Education Conference at the University of Nottingham, England. The conference was hosted by Women Leading in Education Across Continents (WLE). The theme was "Ways of seeing women's leadership in education: stories, images, metaphors, methods, and theories." Several months before the conference, I had been posting tweets about women in education leadership and the importance of well-being. My posts were centered around the data on well-being as a critical factor for women and their ability to be successful and thrive in senior leadership positions.

My tweets got the attention of Dr. Kerry Robinson, associate professor in the Department of Education Leadership at the University of North Carolina Wilmington. Dr. Robinson has written about superintendent stress and health being a factor in longevity and effective leadership. We hold a shared belief that maintaining a thriving well-being in both a woman's personal and professional life is an enormous lift and challenge. Kerry messaged me and suggested we should talk sometime about our mutual interest in this area. I agreed. And a few weeks later, I found myself in my car headed to Wilmington, excited to make her acquaintance.

The evening I arrived, we met for dinner at a wonderful vegan restaurant. Kerry knew we possessed veganism as a shared value. She chose a perfect restaurant to meet. We talked about the challenges and benefits of such a lifestyle. We shared tips and strategies that make such a choice easier. We lingered over dinner as we talked and laughed and shared stories about our professional and personal life. We learned we were both dog lovers and that our four-legged fur babies were beloved members of our families. We talked about our work.

Kerry worked with students aspiring to be school leaders, assistant principals, and principals and she witnessed daily how their well-being was impacted by the systems they are trying to navigate and the very hard work they do. She talked about her students in such a caring way that made clear they were in loving hands. We had a shared mission in seeing women in school leadership positions thrive. We deliberated about and questioned the roadblocks women face, the significant role well-being plays, and what's missing in education leadership programs that women need and are desperately in search of. We agreed that we would explore ways we could partner together around our mutual interest and desire to see more women as school leaders and how to create the conditions for us to thrive.

A few months later, Kerry contacted me about a conference presentation opportunity. We co-wrote an abstract and proposal to present at the WLE Conference. Our topic was going to focus on the well-being of women school leaders. We submitted our proposal and it was accepted. I was thrilled to attend and co-present at the conference along with esteemed women scholars from across five continents who would be there to present their research in the field of women's educational leadership.

I touched down at Heathrow Airport on Sunday, July 7, 2019. Before I left home, I planned out the best travel route to Nottingham. This was the first time I would navigate international travel alone and I was both anxious and excited. I knew it would include a ride on the tube and a train and take me about three hours to arrive at my final destination. I maneuvered through the airport following the signs for the tube. I looked for the Piccadilly Line to King's Cross/St. Pancras. This was a joint station where I would need to change lines. The King's Cross station was bustling with people who all seemed to know where they were going. Inside, the station resembled a food court at a high-end mall. People were everywhere, trying to make their way to their tube or having a meal at one of the many eateries. I searched for the signs that would point me in the direction of the train headed for Nottingham and made my way tugging my very large red suitcase behind me and my black backpack on my shoulders. I found the train headed to Nottingham. Once inside the car, I searched for a comfortable seat by the window and settled in. I let out a big sigh and reveled in my successful journey so far.

This leg of my travels would take almost two hours, so I took out my book and started to read. I waffled between reading and peering out my window. The landscape transitioned between the backyard of homes and open countryside. As I gazed at the homes, I wondered who lived there and how those dwellings might be different from the ones in the United States. The time passed quickly, and I arrived on time in Nottingham. I clumsily retrieved my big red suitcase, flung my backpack over my shoulder, and made my way through the station. Once outside, I found a driver who would help me complete my journey. It was a quick car ride to the University of Nottingham. As the driver pulled up to the entrance of the campus hotel, I silently basked in my successful journey from Heathrow to Nottingham. No matter what else happened over the next four days, I would feed off the success of my journey.

Upon arriving at the University of Nottingham, I immediately realized this was going to be a different kind of conference experience. After we checked into our rooms, we gathered for an opening cocktail reception. The ceiling of the hotel atrium had skylights that invited the sun to radiate throughout the room, creating a warm feel and glow. You could see the clouds of dust swirling in the streams of sunlight. At the end of the room were large glass doors with a view of a glistening pond and flowing fountain. There was a large deck outside where we could sit and take in the view. A bar was set up in the center of the lobby and a table with finger foods and small appetizers for us to enjoy after our long day of travel. Right away, I noticed this was not the first experience at this event for many of the attendees. They greeted each other with warmth and enthusiasm, the way best girlfriends do after not having seen one another for a very long time. I was new to the group and knew only Kerry. But I was welcomed with kind words and open arms.

I ordered a glass of wine and filled my plate with food. I got comfortable on one of the many cozy chairs and couches placed throughout the room. We introduced ourselves to one another, asked questions, provided answers, and began our three-day journey together, longing to discover how we could make school leadership better for ourselves, one another, and millions of women not in attendance. All the participants and presenters were brilliant, amazing women from all over the world. Most came from higher education either as grad students or professors. After a few words of welcome from our conference host, we wrapped up our conversations and retreated to our rooms. Most of us had long journeys that day, and we were exhausted. I know I was after hauling that big red suitcase and my backpack through two stations. We all wanted to be at our very best and rested for the presentations, discussions, and continued networking and connecting that was ahead of us.

The next morning, we met back in the lobby, the same place where the reception had been held the night before. We all boarded buses that transported us to the conference room where we would hold up together for the next three days. Some of the women wore a traditional, customary dress from their countries. They were breathtaking in the bright yellows, oranges, blues, and greens of the fabric. Some were dressed in business attire, and some, like me, were dressed comfortably so as not to be distracted by high-heeled shoes or how we must sit. The exuberance continued as the women greeted each other, hugged the ones who arrived late past our happy hour, and continued the conversations they were having the prior evening.

Let me give you a sense of the uniqueness in the design of this conference. The room where we met over the three days was of modest size and space was reserved upfront for the presenters, so we were all pretty snug and seated close to one another. The closeness felt like a warm blanket being wrapped around you. This was unlike most conferences, where we are traditionally seated at large round banquet tables spread across mammoth ballrooms. There was no need for us to show up early to find that perfect spot where we would face the speaker or screen. We could all see and hear one another just fine. The room size did not require a microphone, although one was available. This allowed presenters to connect with everyone in the room through their own voices and not that of the muffled or raspy sounds of a large PA system. It lent to the intimacy of the gathering.

Time was not wasted in traveling from break-out room to break-out room. Rather we spent all our time gathered together and engaged in lively, deep meaningful conversation. Priya Parker, professional facilitator and author of the best-selling book *The Art of Gathering*, says, "Gatherings crackle and flourish when real thought goes into them, when (often visible) structure is baked into them, and when a host has the curiosity, willingness, and generosity of spirit to try."[2] This was more than a conference—it was a gathering. And we continued this way throughout the three days we were together.

All participants, over sixty of us, would remain in the same room. The presenters were clustered into groups according to research abstract topics. There was no list of sessions we would need to plow through and decide to attend. There was no remorse in trying to be at two sessions at the same time as many topics interested us. We remained assembled together in the one intimate conference room for the entire day. Most of the participants sat at tables with four or six other women. Some were seated in chairs in the back of the room. I remained at a table with the same three women the entire time.

Each presenter had approximately fifteen minutes to share her study, data, findings, and conclusions. It was like speed dating, except it was speed presenting. Nearly every woman scholar presented her research on issues pertaining to women's leadership. Some of the topics included historical perspectives, gender and intersectionality challenges, the impact of various methods of leadership, and women's networks and activism. I loved that almost all the data gathered was qualitative. Women were telling and sharing

---

2   Priya Parker, *The Art of Gathering: How We Meet and Why It Matters* (Penguin USA, 2020).

their stories. That meant what we were listening to was a collection of lived experiences by women in the field.

After all members of a common topic group had spoken, they formed a panel and we were able to ask questions. There was a timekeeper for both the individual presentations and the panel discussion. The timekeeper kept everyone on track. This generated presentations and panel discussions that were succinct, fast-paced, and high-energy with the lack of extraneous slides and saturation of a similar theme. I loved everyone being in the same room. It reminded me of the lyrics from the Broadway musical Hamilton, "No one else was in the room where it happened. The room where it happened." No one else except sixty-five brilliant, courageous, wonderful women were in that room. The small groups at tables made for nuanced conversations that built relationships and connections. This wasn't just a conference. This was a powerful gathering.

A Black woman from the UK sat at my table, and we instantly bonded. She introduced herself. For the purpose of this story, we will call her Anita. We both described where we worked and what we did. I shared how this was my first experience at a WEL conference, that I was presenting on the final day, and how I was a bit nervous as I was not a researcher. She asked me to describe my abstract. I explained how I was planning to present the five elements of well-being as defined in the Gallup research and the impact on women. And we were off in conversation. She asked me questions about how I defined well-being. What was the difference, as I saw it, between well-being and wellness? How can we incorporate well-being into a leadership practice? Why was focusing on well-being so imperative for women? How does well-being relate to leadership? Her questions were encouraging, and I greatly appreciated her genuine interest in my topic.

I answered. I asked her about her experience as a university educator and professor in the UK. She graciously explained the UK higher education structure and how in most ways it was similar to the United States. She thoughtfully shared the differences between the two systems. I listened intently to learn. She worked at the University College of London in the education institute. She also shared how after WEL she would be chairing a conference a few hours away. She was active in BELMAS, British Educational Leadership, Management & Administration Society. She was an education activist dedicated to making positive change and ensuring equity and equality. I knew I liked her!

She shared with me the lens through which she would be listening to the presentations and what she was anticipating hearing from every presenter. As the scholars would speak she would listen to confirm similar or vastly different stories of Black women. She was looking for similar lived experiences. Or the contrary. And she was hopeful the women would present all points of view. She would also call out when those experiences were not included or were missing altogether in the data. She would help me understand when Black women were represented and when they were not.

As one of the presenters flipped through her slides, I heard Anita give out an audible "Ugh."

I turned toward her and gave a look that said, "Please explain. What am I not seeing?"

The slide was meant to represent data about young girls. The images were all of White girls. She helped me understand what it meant to her to not see faces that represented all girls and her frustration with the speaker that she was not aware of the lack of representation in her images. I could see the pain and frustration on her face. After all, this was an international conference for and about women with attendees from all over the world representing the diaspora of Blackness. It was as though Anita had taken off my metaphorical glasses and wiped them down with a clean cloth in order to improve my vision. It was amazing how she helped me see clearer and in color, all color. It was a clear memory of my unwrapping.

I was starting to understand the lived experiences of women are not all the same. We are not monolithic. Black, Brown, Indigenous, Asian, and Non-Binary women are often left out of the narrative, and when we refer to "women's issues," generally, we center them around White women. I will forever be grateful for my honest conversations with this vulnerable, courageous woman from the UK I call Anita.

I settled into this cozy room beside my new friend and listened to all the extraordinary women scholars. On this very first day, I already began to notice a pattern. Whether they were discussing the challenges and obstacles for women in education to enter leadership, remain in their position, or rise to higher levels on the leadership ladder, the overall universal barrier was both similar and unique. In Nigeria, women education leaders face structural and systemic issues just like in the United States and around the world. Although in their country they are represented in number, women continue to suffer in their well-being due to societal and self-made demands on their role and status. The patriarchy that exists, gender inequality, and lack of pursuing positions by women result in a loss of diverse gender talent in schools and higher education. These issues are not unique to Nigeria, but the details are unique to their culture.

As one presenter after another discussed her research findings, it slowly became clear, frustrating, and painful that the collective struggle women have in obtaining and remaining in leadership positions is comparable. It also appears our collective struggle is born with obstacles specific to regions, cultures, and communities. The intersectionality of gender and race cannot be denied. It is universal no matter what country or culture women derive from. Leadership spaces still tend to be dominated by men—and in the US, White men— microaggressions are ignored or accepted, and the voices and opinions of women are silenced or ignored. In White-dominated countries, Black, Indigenous, and Women of Color are marginalized. I discovered the factors that impact women in Brazil were not exactly the same as in the Philippines. The specific issues that affect women in India are not the same as the issues in the United States. Women face issues that are unique to their place of origin. Women in leadership also face challenges and opportunities that are universal. If I placed the issues that surfaced in the studies I heard that first day under a microscope, the challenge of maintaining a thriving and happy life would be revealed. Well-being matters. The well-being of women matters.

I returned to my room after the first day of presentations with two thoughts. How am I to lead a presentation here with all these brilliant women scholars? And did I have enough to say that they would want to hear, that would matter or make a difference? I was one of the only presenters who did not come from higher education and who did not have a PhD after her name. I was a bit intimidated, to say the least. That gremlin who appears from time to time and sits on my shoulder and whispers, "You can't do this. What are you thinking? Who do you think you are?" Women make friends with that gremlin, and it appears whenever we want to do something audacious, courageous, and vulnerable. The gremlin's name is scarcity. It also goes by imposter syndrome.

I had not conducted academic research. In fact, I had not fully completed my presentation. The plan I described to Anita was to present research and data on well-being and to define the impact it has on our life and work. To show how well-being saturated the studies presented at this conference. And then to provide specific ways to operationalize well-being as a leadership practice. She assured me it was what the attendees would want to hear. She shared it was what she needed to hear. She reminded me I was not scheduled to present until the final day and by then they would have their fill of research and data. They will be hungry for what to do next and what actions they can take when they return home. I could provide that for them.

Was that enough for this conference and these attendees? The plan was for Dr. Robinson to introduce me then I would lead the presentation and the discussion. I scrupulously reread my notes from all the presentations I heard that day. Patterns began to emerge around obstacles women face. These barriers appeared over and over again in the data from the various studies. I was eager to test my hypothesis and listen for similar findings during the next round of presentations.

The morning of the second day was sunny and spring-like. We gathered together once again in the atrium waiting for the bus to transport us to our snug conference room. The morning sunlight once again poured its way through the large windows in the open lobby and rested on the chairs and tables. The sun would dance and move during the day and look different when we returned in the late afternoon. The drive through the University of Nottingham campus was beautiful. We meandered down tree-lined roads, past fountains, and small lakes to our building where we would gather once again.

I greeted my new friend, Anita, and told her how grateful I was for our conversation yesterday and that I was looking forward to spending another day with her. On this day, I was listening to the speakers with intention. I was keen on testing my hypothesis.

I chatted with Anita about what I was thinking and asked if she would debrief with me later about what she'd heard. She kindly agreed to do so. As the presentations continued, I observed no one fully defining the issues that women leaders jointly shared. They were more focused on their research process and outcomes. The women scholars from Brazil talked about living in a strong patriarchal, religious culture and tradition while navigating the responsibilities of their leader position at school and on campus. Women from Sadia Arabia revealed how their research showed women leaders struggle with breaking the glass ceiling. They could climb the ladder of leadership only to be prevented from climbing to the top. And the presenters from various countries in Africa discussed their data on gender bias in leader identification.

I began to think of my own experience in unison and in unity with what I was hearing. I began thinking about my own struggle to balance a well-lived life along with my professional responsibilities. When I was traveling several times a month for my work at Gallup, I would begin prepping for my trip days in advance. I would make a casserole, cover it in tin foil, and with a permanent marker, write the baking directions on top. This way, I knew my husband and two young daughters would have a healthy meal. In reality, it was a way to appease my conditioned guilt of leaving them for two or three days. I would write a dissertation for my husband to include an hour-by-hour schedule of my daughters' activities, who I arranged to pick them up, and how they would get home. It was my attempt to keep the peace at home while I left to do the work I so loved doing. During this mad process, I often wondered how many men bake casseroles for their wives and leave a diary of carpool instructions before they go on a business trip—another example of the critical need to look behind the curtain of women's well-being and social conditioning as they progress in their chosen professions. Another way to become unwrapped.

I think women are all like ducks. We look calm, cool, and collected on top of the water in our black and navy suits and heels when in reality, we are paddling like hell underneath. As I continued to listen to the speakers, I was reminded of my own painful experiences with patriarchy, misogyny, favoritism, and my struggles to maintain a thriving well-being in a workplace culture that made it nearly impossible. It was on the second day of the conference I decided on the topic of my presentation. I would take their findings and make them practical and operational. I checked in with Anita. Sought her experience and counsel. When she affirmed my idea and insights, I decided definitively I would gather all the studies under a framework of well-being for women.

I went back to my room on the second evening and knew exactly what I would talk about and from what perspective. I spent over sixteen years as a consumer of research and data as an education consultant and one of my strengths has always been to tell the data story and to operationalize findings to drive impact and behavioral change. That is what I intended to do in my conference presentation. I would present to the group from a data consumer's lens, show them the commonalities in their studies, and how what their studies exposed can be used to drive change for women. I would spell out how I had been suffering in my purpose well-being. And share that when we suffer in our purpose we show up at work differently, are incapable of using our strengths in a productive and healthy way, and behave in a way that is out of alignment with our values.

Defining what we mean by well-being is critical for women leaders, and to those we lead. Too many bad leadership decisions are made due to suffering well-being. Those being led by suffering leaders bear the weight of those bad decisions. When I returned to my room that evening, I put together my "speed presentation," pulled findings from studies presented over the past two days, and illustrated how I would operationalize the data to create leadership practices women can employ to thrive in their roles. I would be sure my slides represented *all* women as Anita made me so clearly aware. My presentation was designed to be the arch of the conference. We had heard from so many scholars about the challenges but not how to address them. This would be my scholarly contribution to a most unique and memorable conference.

Presenting the data on well-being to over sixty brilliant and capable women leaders was especially meaningful and personal for me. I would channel all that emotion and my own trauma into my delivery. I knew my suffering well-being was the chief reason I needed to leave my job at Gallup. I needed to share my story of caution and commonality. I had been suffering in my "purpose" well-being. When we suffer in this way, we show up at work differently than who we are at our core; it's difficult to choose and practice authenticity, and we default to what is acceptable and centered. It's easier to fall into the expectations of others to fit in. That was me at that time. I wanted to send up the brightest flares of warning to these women and give them a foundation in which to include well-being as a human leadership practice.

The last day arrived, July 11, 2019. It was my turn to speak. Dr. Robinson told our crazy story of how we met through Twitter, had a wonderful vegan meal together, and submitted the abstract that was selected to be presented at this event. She shared a little about me and then handed the presentation over for me to lead and deliver. I walked the participants through what I heard was the common thread in all the studies and stories they had collected. I specifically defined well-being and explained why it mattered. I gave them an action plan they could take home with them to begin making their well-being the foundation of a thriving leadership practice. I delivered my "speed presentation," and it stood out as being unique from all the others. That was my intention. I wanted my words to be memorable, understandable, and useful to every woman listening.

My last slide was a photo of a diverse group of women. I looked over at Anita and saw her big smile. I winked at her to say, "I listened, and I heard you, my new friend." After I completed my last slide, there was roaring applause, an indication that what I had chosen to present was on point and resonated with the women in the room. During the panel discussion, I was asked about my data. I shared the data I used from Gallup but also reminded them that I referenced the studies conducted by the very people in the room. All those stories matter. I was asked questions about how to employ well-being in their leadership practice, how school and district leaders can begin to include well-being as a critical component of their culture. The women shared more anecdotes about their own well-being and how they struggle or suffer. I knew I hit a nerve. Their questions told me they heard my message. And I hoped I sent the message that I heard their stories. This was my "scholarly" contribution to the conference and hopefully a gift to the women in the room. Well-being for women education leaders matters.

When I think back on my experience at Gallup, I can now look at it through the lens of well-being. The decision to leave my role and the workplace culture that existed at that time was a well-being decision. I continue to be a believer and devoted patron of the science, research, and data the scientists at Gallup uncover on thriving workplaces and cultures. They have some of the best research on well-being, what it is, and the impact on people or a community. They define well-being as the "essential currency of a life that matters"[3]

Tom Rath, a consultant on employee engagement, strengths, and well-being and best-selling author, external advisor, and Gallup Senior Scientist states, "well-being is about the combination of our love for what we do each day, the quality of our relationships, the security of our finances, the vibrancy of our physical health and the pride we take in what we have contributed to our communities. Most importantly, it's about how these five elements interact." Gallup has been exploring the impact of well-being for decades. Together with economists, psychologists, researchers, and scientists, they expose the differences between a thriving life and one where individuals struggle or suffer.[4] The scientists identified the "currency of a life that matters." Their research identifies five elements that contribute to thriving well-being. As I thought about well-being and the impact on women, I dissected each of the elements to determine how they show up in our lives and the impact on women in leadership.

> **Purpose:** Purpose well-being for women in education is their job, career, where they go to spend most of their day. When we are thriving in our purpose well-being, we are at our best for colleagues, staff, teachers, parents, and families we serve and work with daily

> **Social:** Social well-being refers to having loving, healthy relationships in our life. This includes our partners, families, friends, colleagues, and members of our work and social community. When women are thriving in social well-being,

---

3   James K. Harter et al., "The Relationship Between Engagement at Work And Organizational Outcomes," (Gallup, February 2013), https://employeeengagement.com/wp-content/uploads/2013/04/2012-Q12-Meta-Analysis-Research-Paper.pdf.
4   Ibid.

we are in healthy relationships where there is reciprocity in giving and receiving. In this area, we often fall back into the roles we have learned through social conditioning. This fallback can cause us to suffer in this area.

Financial: We are efficient about our finances and resources, and we are managing them well. This is an area that ebbs and flows throughout our personal and professional lives. As school budgets affect salaries, we must be aware of how that impacts our financial well-being.

Physical: Physical well-being is how well we eat healthily, get enough sleep, and move daily to be able to achieve and accomplish all we desire to do. Women, in general, too often succumb to a social view of their physical well-being and spend their financial resources and time on achieving what others believe to be the ideal in physical well-being. We must define this for ourselves.

Community: How connected are you to your community? Do you belong to and are active in an organization that serves your community, a church, and/or a social group? A healthy and positive connection to the community matters.

These elements must be considered within the circumstances and conditions of one's life. To cultivate a thriving well-being, women must put all five elements in the context of each individual's lived experience at work, in the community, and at home. Patriarchy, misogyny, systemic racism, and White supremacy culture are experienced not only at work but also in places women move throughout their days and lives. Take the pay gap as an example of suffering financial well-being. In 2019, working women in general in the United States were paid 82 cents for every dollar earned by a man.

Black women suffer a wider pay gap than White women. In 2019, the American Association of University Women (AAUW) reported that Black women must work seven additional months to make the same pay as men. The report goes on to say, "According to the US Census, on average, Black women were paid 63% of what non-Hispanic White men were paid in 2019. That means it takes the typical Black woman nineteen months to be paid what the average White man takes home in twelve months. That's even worse than the national earnings ratio for all women, 82%."[5]

The impact of pay on well-being doesn't just impact the financial element. Because of the integrative feature of well-being, it can also affect purpose, community, physical, and social well-being. The consequences of these disparities affect women in their attempt to create a life well-lived. Women leaders—in fact, all school, district, and campus leaders—should include a well-being reflection as part of their daily leadership practice. It should be taught as a foundational component in all education leadership programs. It matters for women and can be a retention strategy. Our well-being is a leading indicator and impactor on our success and longevity in the position. Creating a thriving workplace culture, one where everyone, including you, has the potential to be successful and achieve goals and outcomes must include a foundation of well-being.

There are many factors that contribute to the suffering well-being of women. In their best-selling book *Burnout, The Secret to Unlocking the Stress Cycle,* Dr. Emily Nagoski and her twin sister Amelia Nagoski provided research-based causes, effects, and solutions to completing the stress cycle. They described three causes of stress and burnout for women including chronic stressors, social appropriateness, and safety. Simply put, the sisters teach us that

5   "Black Women & The Pay Gap," AAUW, September 14, 2021, https://www.aauw.org/resources/article/black-women-and-the-pay-gap/.

when we begin to feel burnout or stress, we often get caught in a cycle or tunnel. A chronic stressor and chronic stress are when we continually return to that which is causing our pain, anxiety, and burnout. A work environment like the one I was experiencing was my chronic stressor. Nothing was changing, yet I returned every single day with the hope that it would. Unhealthy relationships and social well-being—whether at work or in your personal life—contribute to your spiraling stress cycle. It's like returning to the scene of the crime, over and over.

The Nagoski sisters teach us about *human savior syndrome.* Women are socialized to believe that it is our moral obligation and imperative to be in constant service to others, always, and to be in a continuous state of giving. It made me think about how I used to make the casseroles for my family when I went on business trips and wrote those long narratives of instructions on how to raise our girls while I was gone. The thing is, that casserole was always in the refrigerator untouched when I returned. And my daughters were alive and well. We need not look any further than the impact of the pandemic. Data from McKinsey & Company shows the impact of the pandemic has been a heavier burden on women.[6] Women have taken on an unequal share of the burden of childcare, teaching, and schooling during our collective lockdown. Women have experienced the greatest economic loss or downfall as we gave up our means of financial well-being to attend to needs at home. We do this with no concern for ourselves.

Our collective struggling or suffering well-being is the result of our never-ending efforts to thrive in systems that were not created

---

6   Anu Madgavkar et al., "Covid-19 and Gender Equality: Countering the Regressive Effects," McKinsey & Company (McKinsey & Company, April 10, 2021), https://www.mckinsey.com/featured-insights/future-of-work/covid-19-and-gender-equality-countering-the-regressive-effects.

by us or for us. Schools are founded on a patriarchal system; to be more specific, white male power and authority. Women spend all their time trying to fit in rather than belong. In a 2018 journal article from *Phi Delta Kappan*, the authors write about the origin of women in school leadership. They describe one of our greatest challenges as the "gendered career system."[7]

As I researched the history of leadership in education, I discovered leadership positions became more professionalized over time and the norms and skill sets associated with the best candidates for principal and superintendent came from men who either went back to school using the GI Bill or had experience as an athletic coach. Women, however, became specialists in curriculum and instruction. These were skills preferred for those who supported teachers inside the school but not for the leader. "It seemed to be the natural order of things that women taught and men managed."[8] The skill sets men acquired as coaches were perceived as more preferable in managing a staff and budgets. This was, and remains, especially true at the high school level, where large community involvement exists and the success of athletic programs is highly favored. Women continue to fight and work our way out of this norm and prototype.

The authors also point out that school boards, their priorities in governing, and gender bias in hiring posed another obstacle for women who want to lead. Data shows school boards spend more time discussing budgets, athletics, construction, safety, and transportation than the "invisible" activity of teaching and learning. The exact place where women shine and hold expertise. And when they do get involved in issues inside the classroom it is often for political

---

7   Robert Maranto et al., "Boys Will Be Superintendents: School Leadership as a Gendered Profession," kappanonline.org, October 3, 2018, https://kappanonline.org/maranto-carroll-cheng-teodoro-school-leadership-gender/.

8   Ibid, p, 102.

purposes and control. Our social conditioning and expectations around being the caretaker at home have made remaining in the classroom more attractive to women and better able to manage a home and work balance. In reality, this is a fallacy as teaching has become more and more complex and demanding and another example of why well-being matters for women who desire to pursue a leadership position.

Expectations of what it means to be an effective school or district leader must change until social norms change. The authors submit there are several ways to address these issues: one, reform the hierarchical structure of school leadership, two, address the perpetuation of outdated thinking and habits of local school boards, three, examine the requirement of needing to obtain a doctorate to become a principal or superintendent as many women are challenged with time and mentorship in which to complete one.

I submit there is a fourth way to reverse this trend. Women can begin to practice that fierce self-compassion described by Dr. Kristin Neff and speak up, tell their stories, and ask for what they need and want. In her book, *Fierce Self-Compassion: How Women Can Harness Kindness to Speak Up, Claim Their Power, and Thrive,* Dr. Neff tells us in her introduction, "Traditional gender roles and societal power structures restrict the ability of women to express the full range of who we are, at great cost both personally and politically. Women are allowed to be soft, nurturing, and tender. But if a woman is too fierce—if we're too angry and forceful—people get scared and call us names (witch, hag, shrew, and ball-breaker are some of the milder insults that come to mind). If we're ever going to move beyond male dominance and take our proper place at the tables of power, we need to reclaim the right to be fierce."[9]

---

9   Kristin Neff. *Fierce Self Compassion, How Women Can Harness Kindness to Speak Up, Claim Their Power, and Thrive.* (New York, NY: Harper Wave, 2021).

That begins by obtaining the skill sets and words we currently do not receive in traditional leadership development programs and need to be able to have our voices heard and to constructively disrupt systems. Women leaders have been waiting too long for someone to change the system on our behalf. If we are ever to shatter the glass ceiling in education, we must be the ones to not just shatter it but to raise it so more women can rise to leadership positions and thrive in those roles.

When I reflect back on the class I took in college on the history and foundations of education, I recall how teaching was designed with mostly women in mind. It was considered an extension of our natural "feminine" skill to nurture and raise children. Women initially were also considered the "natural" leader for schools, it evolved to be this way to keep pay low. As men began to choose education leadership and the number of men in those positions increased, the ideal "leader" began to change. And the "prototype" for principal and superintendent became male. Every element of the system including job descriptions, requirements, role models for the ideal school leader, and support were centered around being male, White, cisgendered, married with a wife to support home and child-rearing responsibilities. School districts began to see a decline in the number of women leaders.

In the 2018 *Kappan* article, the authors write, "The numbers of women in school and district leadership declined through most of the 20th century. For example, the percentage of elementary school principal posts held by women fell from 55% in 1928 to 20% in 1973."[10] In the same article, the authors highlight the words of Kate Rousmaniere from her social history of the principalship,

---

10   Robert Maranto et al., "Boys Will Be Superintendents: School Leadership as a Gendered Profession," kappanonline.org, October 3, 2018, https://kappanonline.org/maranto-carroll-cheng-teodoro-school-leadership-gender/.

she notes, "It seemed to be the natural order of things that women taught and men managed."[11] The numbers have begun to rise slowly. Too slowly!

So what is to be done? The system of schooling must be disrupted or we will continue to struggle and suffer and will never realize the breathtaking and effective contributions more women leaders can and will make to impact the experience teachers, staff, students, and families have in our schools. We must begin to tell our story and share our diverse lived experiences. These stories begin to identify the barriers to success and the needs of women leaders. We must start asking for what we need. In order to do so, we must disrupt the traditional leadership development programs and replace them with ones that focus on issues specific to women leaders. These programs must go beyond mentoring, networking, and gathering.

And we have to hold school boards accountable for hiring women senior leaders and creating the conditions in which women leaders at all levels can thrive. We start with taking control of our well-being, identifying the feedback that matters and that serves to make our work better, including a well-being check every day, and practicing the research-based strategies that allow us to move completely through our stress to rise stronger and better to lead on the other side of the stress tunnel. Again from Dr. Neff, "Tender self-compassion harnesses the energy of nurturing to alleviate suffering, while fierce self-compassion harnesses the energy of action to alleviate suffering - when these are fully integrated, they manifest as a caring force."[12] She goes on to say that women must first harness that internal self-compassion so that we can harness our

---

11   Ibid, 102.

12   Kristin Neff. *Fierce Self Compassion, How Women Can Harness Kindness to Speak Up, Claim Their Power, and Thrive.* (New York, NY: Harper Wave, 2021).

fierce self-compassion and advocate for others and social justice, fight against patriarchy and decolonize our cultures, and remain aligned to our values.

So there you have it. Our individual well-being matters. Our collective well-being matters. And although self-kindness and care are essential practices that nurture our well-being it isn't sufficient. What appears in the research over and over again is one of the main causes women in education do not apply for positions of leadership and remain over a long period of time is a suffering well-being. Well-being impacts self-selecting into leadership as our career progresses. No amount of mentoring or collective gatherings will create the conditions where we have a chance to thrive. Systems and cultures must be changed. We start with ourselves in making well-being a leadership practice and teaching it in women-focused professional development.

But there is another area we must address. And that is with the school boards and governing bodies that make leadership hiring decisions. Just because a woman might not do the job exactly like the male principal or superintendent that came before her, that does not mean she is not as equally effective or better and can make a positive impact on the community.

We have defined well-being according to Gallup's data, we have helped you recognize the impacts on your well-being based on data and research, and we have encouraged you to make your well-being a central part of your leadership practice. It is up to us as individuals and as a collective to disrupt the systems that make us unhealthy, oppress us, marginalize our voices, and prevent us from showing up authentically. For if we do not show up authentically and powerfully and own who we are as women leaders, then our only choice is to hustle to fit in, morph into the leader prototype, and scam our way to acceptance. And we will never move the numbers.

What's Your Story?

Questions to ponder as you become unwrapped.

1. How can you incorporate well-being as a leadership practice?

2. In which elements of well-being are you "thriving, surviving, or suffering," as Gallup mentions?

   a. Purpose well-being

   b. Social well-being

   c. Financial well-being

   d. Physical well-being

   e. Community well-being

3. How do your lived experiences impact your well-being?

4. How can you lead with a well-being lens for others, especially other women?

5. What is impacting your well-being? What is in your control to change or shift?

6. Boundary-setting is essential for a thriving well-being. Do you set healthy boundaries for yourself at work and at home? How do you do it? What words do you use? Where do you struggle in setting boundaries?

Strategies and tools you already know. Now use them with a well-being lens.

- Journal—Reflect on the five elements of well-being and rate how you are doing. Begin to make this a weekly practice.

IN SEARCH OF THE TRUTH

Truth is powerful and it prevails.

— Sojourner Truth

SHE ENTERED MY office, angry with narrowed red eyes. She did not understand why the students needed to attend the field trip to Harvard and Princeton. I explained that I wanted the students to experience things outside of the Harlem neighborhood. I wanted them to see that they can go to these Ivy League schools.

She sucked her teeth. "Why are you trying to make them White?"

That comment stung. In fact, I was offended that she would think that I was selling out my students and my school for White norms. What parents wouldn't want their children to go to an Ivy League school? Initially, I dismissed the comment as misinformed, but it stuck with me like a strong adhesive—sticky and annoying. I thought she would understand what I was doing to help my students succeed, but years later and through lots of self-discovery, I learned that I was trying to help them navigate White spaces and fit in so they would be accepted. I was projecting my values of acceptance and assimilation on them. I even named the homerooms after Ivy League schools.

Why didn't I choose Historically Black Colleges (HBCUs)? What message was I sending to my students about what success looks like? The parent was right, and I did not see it until I began working in majority-White, male-dominated environment and realized my climb. My search to unwrap the truth begins.

Authenticity

What does it mean to "be real"? I was taught that there was a certain way that I needed to behave with friends that were different from the way that I behave at work or among elders. Does the switch in behavior mean that I am not being authentic? I ask again, what does it mean to "be real?"

Numerous research articles, books, and podcasts have explored the concept of showing up "authentically you," and most of the work is geared toward women and women of color because of the historical misogyny, patriarchal, and racists environments in which we work that stifle our ability to courageously "lean in" and make our voices heard without retribution or retaliation. Part of being authentic means understanding what authentic means.

Let's break down the word first. According to Webster's dictionary, *authentic* means "of undisputed origin; genuine." In today's digital world, we are so bombarded by images of beauty and behavioral norms that it is hard to determine what is real. As a young adult, I would laugh at women who had fake nails, hair, boobs, and asses. I would think, *How could they do that to themselves?* Especially as I watched celebrities transform their skin, noses, waistlines, and so on, I often wondered what they saw in the mirror that forced them to transform their look. What did they see?

Yet I excused myself from these questions, even though I straightened my hair, dressed a certain way, and "acted" in ways that were acceptable. I may not have made drastic physical transformations, but my mindset fed the story that I needed to be something and someone for others so that I could be accepted. My mindset has been molded since I was a little girl, by my mother, grandmother, my experiences in school, college, and work. My beliefs, values, and perspectives are shaped by these experiences. They are not bad. They were the ways that helped me survive a harsh world, especially for a young Black girl from the South Bronx. The main objective was to fit in—be accepted by peers, strangers, and society.

As I reflected on my life, I realized that I was no different from the people I criticized. I was perpetrating a false narrative. Peeling the layers requires courage and as an educational leader and especially a woman in leadership, all eyes are on you. In my current work, these layers are my protection, shielding the constant real or perceived blows of criticism, shame, and micro/macro-aggressions. The toggle back and forth between the unwrapped you and the shielded you are constant.

Much has been written about the place and role of the woman and the Black woman in history. Much of the structures and ideas persist today. One of the most notable historical events that thrust the intersection of gender and race in the women's rights movement was the Ohio Women's Rights Convention in 1851. Sojourner Truth, in her fierce confidence, declared, "Ain't I a woman?" Sojourner Truth, born Isabella Buamfree, endured the unspeakable horrors of slavery. It was recorded that she was sold four times before running away in 1827 with her infant daughter to abolitionists who bought her freedom.[13] She settled in New York City in 1828 and began her recovery and spiritual revival. After being

---

13   Edited by Debra Michals, "Sojourner Truth," Biography: Sojourner truth (National Women's History Museum, 2015), https://www.womenshistory.org/education-resources/biographies/sojourner-truth.

touched by the Spirit, she changed her name to Sojourner Truth and began to minister and speak her truth. The story of Sojourner Truth's journey to physical, psychological, and spiritual freedom resonates because she knew that race and gender had to be tackled simultaneously, especially for Black women.

In her speech to the men and women at the Women's Rights Convention, she fiercely stated,

> *That man over there says that women need to be helped into carriages, and lifted over ditches, and to have the best place everywhere. Nobody ever helps me into carriages, or over mud-puddles, or gives me any best place! And ain't I a woman? Look at me! Look at my arm! I have ploughed and planted, and gathered into barns, and no man could head me! And ain't I a woman? I could work as much and eat as much as a man - when I could get it - and bear the lash as well! And ain't I a woman? I have borne thirteen children, and seen most all sold off to slavery, and when I cried out with my mother's grief, none but Jesus heard me! And ain't I a woman? ... If the first woman God ever made was strong enough to turn the world upside down all alone, these women together ought to be able to turn it back, and get it right side up again!*[14]

I hear her conviction, determination, and her call to arms to all women. Sojourner became a significant voice in the abolitionist and women's suffrage movement. Her personal narrative tends to be minimized. Truth evolved, stripped the bonds of slavery, and fought racist, patriarchal structures including clashing with Frederick Douglass and William Lloyd Garrison. Additionally, she was one of the few Blacks to sue a White slave owner and win for the

14   Sojourner Truth. "Ain't I a Woman" Speech, Delivered at the Women's Convention, Akron, Ohio. 1851.

return of her son who had been sold into slavery. These minimized stories, and others like Harriet Tubman, are important to understand the power of a freed mind and love of the authentic self. You are willing to fight for your soul.

Sojourner fiercely declared, "If women want any rights more than they's got, why don't they just take them, and not be talking about it."

I am in search of my truth, my authenticity. Being authentic requires the act of self-discovery. It means stripping away the layers of masks and personas that become so much a part of my life. And it is hard to determine what is real and what is a mask. Here is the good news! We are destined to be ourselves. That is why there is always this longing for peace, an unsettling feeling in our mind, body, and soul that tells us that we are not whole.

You see, wearing the masks and transforming ourselves regularly is exhausting. Imagine changing your clothes five to six times a day to accommodate someone's ideal of what is acceptable. Then, align your dress with specific types of behavioral norms to fit the outfits. Finally, each day, the outfits are different so that there is no consistent pattern. You can see how living in this constant state of change and masking can be draining. There comes a time when we are burned out. On these days, we throw up our hands, and say, "Fuck it!" This is the true self.

The fuck-it self is as close to who we are authentically. Don't you notice how freeing it is? It is like taking off the bra and wearing those comfy pajamas all day. We lounge in them. We don't care that they may be ripped or even smell because they have not been washed. You feel secure in them and they are the perfect fit because they are loose and unrestrictive. You wish you could wear them every day. You dread having to change and then you realize you do not want people seeing you like this so the authentic self is short-lived and you go back to wearing the mask and starting the draining routine again.

All of this is driven by fear. Fear of what people might say or do when we show up as ourselves. And this fear is both real and perceived. This is my rat race! In environments where we are few or "onlys," the survival strategy is on full display. As women, we acquiesce to the norms, roles, and stereotypes prescribed and at times, use them to "climb the ladder of success" within an organization or school district. Being bold and decisive may be attractive on the outside, but the sentiment at the water cooler or teacher's lounge is that she is bitchy or mean. She could be mean but is this the same sentiment given to men?

The fear of being you is so strong that even when the environment is safe, we convince ourselves that it is not and we revert to prescribed identities. Damn, this is a masterful design and indicative of the seasoning tactics used on enslaved Africans. The "seasoning" was the physical, social-emotional, and psychological abuse tactics used to condition enslaved people to the new land. These included separating families, restricting food, renaming, undressing, and other abusive treatment to ensure that enslaved Africans did not run away or revolt. Often, enslaved men and women would be flogged or lynched as a reminder of their worth and conditioning. This was social, physical, and psychological warfare. And for generations, it still works. We see it when we make ourselves small or pass up opportunities because we tell ourselves we are not good enough. We even chastise each other to keep us "in line." Again, how do we break free from these social, physical, and psychological chains? It may be necessary to do what Sojourner Truth did when she had enough—the risk and courage to break free.

It is in that moment when Sojourner Truth, in all of her six-foot frame, walked off her slave owner's plantation, in broad daylight with her infant daughter in her arms, and journeyed to freedom.

Real

After the ratification of the Nineteenth Amendment in 1920, which guaranteed American women the right to vote, women continued to fight to exercise their rights as equal to men in this county. Leading women abolitionists and suffragists such as Sojourner Truth, Susan B. Anthony, Harriet Tubman, Elizabeth Caty Stanton, and others paved the way to change the institution of racism and sexism for women and Blacks. Mary McCleod Bethune, one of the most recognized educators of the early 1900s, continued to fight for equality for Black women by building her own college and ensuring that Black women had access and opportunity to one of the most basic rights, education. These women and countless others who we have read about, the unsung sheroes, and those continuing to break barriers illustrate that the fight for equality is far from over. The stories behind the stories provide a historical view of the often purposeful silenced voices of women.

The most recent account of the purposeful silencing of women occurred during the 2020 American vice presidential debate. While then vice-president nominee Kamala Harris was interrupted by Vice President Pence, she had to declare, "I am speaking." *I am speaking!* These words rang through my body like a visceral fingernail scratch on a chalkboard. *I am speaking.* That moment and those words exemplified the struggle of women in patriarchal, misogynistic cultures around the world. From the attempted silencing of Malala Yousafzai to young climate activist Greta Thunberg, and Me Too Movement founder, Tarana Burke. So many women related to that one statement because our voices are typically silenced. To hear her say these words brought forth hundreds of years of oppression in a single moment. *I am speaking!*

In a February 2021 *Washington Post* article written by acclaimed psychologist and author Adam Grant, he revealed data that showed that even though women are typically stereotyped as being talkative, women in leadership speak about 30 percent less than men in meetings or conferences. In fact, he goes on to state that "people expect men to be assertive and ambitious but women to be caring and other-oriented. A man who runs his mouth and holds court is a confident expert. A woman who talks is aggressive or pushy."[15]

These stereotypes run deep in historical legislation that persists today. It was only a hundred years ago that women were "given" the right to vote. Let that sink in. That meant male politicians, elite landowners, agreed that women should have a voice and be seen as valued in the democratic process.

While the passage of the Nineteenth Amendment solidified the rights of women to vote, the practice of voter suppression, especially for Black and indigenous people, was elevated with the introduction of Jim Crow laws in the South to the practice of literacy exams and citizenship identification in the North. Then there were terror tactics—women being burned at the stake and Black men and women brutalized and lynched to silence and reemphasize "their place." Couple this with the extreme oppression and brutality of women who dared to "speak up" and you get a toxic mixture of internal and external taming.

Glennon Doyle describes the phenomenon of "taming" in her book, *Untamed,* as a purposeful structured design to condition women to turn inward and perpetrate an unnatural state. She explains, "We weren't born distrusting and fearing ourselves. That was part of our taming. We were taught to believe that who we are

---

15   Adam Grant, "Perspective | Who Won't Shut up in Meetings? Men Say It's Women. It's Not.," The Washington Post (WP Company, February 18, 2021), https://www.washingtonpost.com/outlook/2021/02/18/men-interrupt-women-tokyo-olympics/.

in our natural state is bad and dangerous. They convinced us to be afraid of ourselves. So we do not honor our own bodies, curiosity, hunger, judgment, experience, or ambition. Instead, we lock away our true selves. Women who are best at this disappearing act earn the highest praise: She is so selfless. Can you imagine? The epitome of womanhood is to lose one's self completely. That is the end goal of every patriarchal culture. Because a very effective way to control women is to convince women to control themselves."[16] This way of being is not sustainable. It is unnatural. This conditioning is taught from home and reinforced in our schools and work environments.

To further explain this notion, Maya Angelou, esteemed author, poet, actress, and singer uses the metaphor of the caged bird throughout her works to describe the oppressive intersectionality of race and gender.

The caged bird sings
with a fearful trill
of things unknown
but longed for still
and his tune is heard
on the distant hill
for the caged bird
sings of freedom.[17]

As women, we long for freedom. We know that it is unnatural to suppress our true selves. That is why we feel the pulling and the longing to break free—be untamed and uncaged. Centuries of

16 Glennon Doyle, *Untamed* (New York, NY: The Dial Press, 2020).
17 Maya Angelou. Excerpt. "Caged Bird" from *Shaker, Don't You Sing?* (New York, NY: Random House, 1983).

physical, emotional, and psychological shackles have conditioned us to shrink, be small, hide in the background and fear the onslaught of abuse. But many women choose courage and set the path for others like me to practice courage.

As an educator, I have the privilege of modeling courageous leadership and I have the scars to prove it. While the field is heavily dominated by women, upper-level and executive leadership positions continue to be dominated by White men. So, the predominant patriarchal ideas continue to permeate the social norms. Schools serve as a microcosm of the social structures. These norms are taught and reinforced through the curriculum content, classroom structure, dress code, sports, and extracurricular activities.

From an early age, girls are tamed:

"Ladies are not loud."

"Girls should not hang out with boys, or they will bring trouble onto themselves."

"Girls are nurturers, caregivers, and emotional beings."

We accept these conditions and shape our lives around these standards. But the yearning for "being more" creeps out from time to time, and we either rebury the "wild" or the "natural," or we are reminded of our place with a stare, scolding, lesson in ladylike decorum, or disassociation by men and women alike. This caging wreaks havoc on our being causing internal scars that we hide with our heads down, a meek smile, or the repeated mantra, "I am fine."

Hey, Mary J. Blige made it an anthem. "I won't change my life, my life's just fine!" Right? I thought I may have been immune from this conditioning, especially growing up around such strong, boisterous women. They encouraged me to speak up, speak out, forge ahead, and don't apologize for who I am and who I will become. And as a young Black girl, it was especially important for me to have a voice. History prepared me to speak up and speak out.

When I was an elementary and middle school teacher, I embodied these values and tried to instill these in my students. As a middle school principal, I continued modeling and preaching these values in hopes that my students would be able to navigate a world where the odds are stacked against them. What I failed to do was teach them to heal the wounds inflicted, practice self-care, and rest. Let some scars heal and lift their head instead of burying the pain and forging ahead. Acknowledge the hurt. Rumble with the pain. Practice recovery. Real meant not showing the pain because that was a sign of weakness but my bones were breaking. How can I stand upright if my insides were withering away?

∽

I kept my head high as I walked with my back straight, my eyes focused down the long hall to my office with the words still echoing in my head.

"I have decided to go with someone else, but I value your commitment to the organization."

Value my commitment? My twelve years of doing everything that was asked of me and more. I sat softly in my chair with a cracked smile on my face. I shuffled some papers on my desk and tried to distract the noise in my head.

Dr. Pethel appeared at the doorway with a soft and comforting smile. I knew that look. The look that one gives when he/she knows something bad but wants to soften the blow. He knew. He grabbed a chair and pulled it up to me and looked at me square in my eyes. He did not say anything, and I did not give him a chance to.

"I am strong. I am strong, Dr. Pethel, but I break. This hurts." That is all I could muster to say as I sobbed. I had never cried for myself at work before. This was the moment when it became real. I spent my career mentoring and coaching students, teachers, and leaders about how to be courageous and navigate challenging situations. I encouraged women to know and speak their worth. I fought, in spirit, for them. I told them that they should not wait to feel and be valued. Find the joy somewhere else or make your own joy.

I never thought I would fall victim to the same stories shared with me. Here I was, head in my hands, wrestling between belief and disbelief. At that moment, I was the most real and raw—a person who was strong, weak, hurt, and empowered. This day marked the start of my recovery to be real.

Perceived

The real fear of authenticity has led to self-imposed restrictions on how to behave or show up in our daily lives. This is akin to an episode of the hit HBO series *Insecure*, where Issa's best friend, Molly, who is a lawyer, tries to tell a new Black employee how she should act at the law firm after seeing her laugh loudly and joke with the other White colleagues. Molly is embarrassed that this new woman is "being herself" and felt it was her duty to share how she should behave in the office around "white folx." Eventually, we see "new girl" in a subsequent scene, muted and small in her disposition.

I remember when this happened to me at work and how I felt after the supposed mentorship. I was in shock! My much older mentor was providing me guidance on how to behave during a meeting at a table full of men. Basically, I was told to write notes and not add anything to the conservation until I was asked. And even when asked, to keep my comments very brief because they are not really interested in my ideas, that the boss already knows what he wants. It was merely a show of inclusion and input gathering.

Wow! What a way to promote the patriarchy! Now, I know that she thought that this advice would spare perceived embarrassment or negative feedback, but I was not afraid of it. The mentorship had an adverse effect. It made me question my value, my ability, and my place within the organization. It led to a level of paranoia I had not experienced in a very long time and this continues with me today. I recall a Forbes article where Dr. Shawn Andrews talked about the "power dead-even rule."[18] Dr. Andrews describes this phenomenon as a way women keep the balance of power. In essence, when there is an imbalance of power and one woman rises in status or position, the other sabotages the rise through public ridicule, degradation, or poor advice to help restore the balance. This is part of unwritten conditioning that women learn as young girls. We see it play out in gossip, rumor, or backstabbing and I was not immune. The situation has become part of my heightened cautious behavior, leading me to question many things before taking action from small things like how to style my hair to how I dress for work.

I recall a fuck-it moment during the summer of 2020. Georgia was under a shelter-in-place order, except for essential workers. As a district employee, I was considered "essential" so I had to report to work daily. The offices were quiet, and the main building was like a ghost town. Many employees were working from home. My house was full with my kids home from college for the summer. My husband was working from home, and work was slow. He was in sales for a large food and catering company. Because colleges were suspending their on-campus dining, his work slowed to almost a complete halt. Days were long, and they busied themselves with cooking, eating, and household games.

---

18   https://www.forbes.com/sites/forbescoachescouncil/2020/01/21/why-women-dont-always-support-other-women/?sh=15fcbd953b05

When I would come home from work, it was as if a bomb had been dropped in the kitchen. Eventually, I joined the mayhem. Why not? It was rare to have everyone at home, and it was an opportunity to reconnect as a family, especially since my youngest son, Justice, was heading to college in the fall. I stopped waking up at 5:15 a.m. and slept for an extra hour. I stopped wearing suits. They were scratchy and restrictive.

And I began wrapping my hair. There was no need to style my hair. I did not want to be bothered by adding a few extra minutes to my morning routine. At first, I was hesitant to do it, hesitant because I had never seen anyone wear any traditional headdress in the twelve years I had been working there, and I was afraid of what people may say. So, one morning I wrapped my head with a traditional kente cloth print and added a pair of African print earrings.

When I walked into the office, my two male counterparts did not say anything except "Good morning." As I met with my team through Zoom, none of the ladies said anything. So, were my fears simply in my mind? Well, it would be tested again later that fall when most people were back in the office, and we hosted our very first back-to-school meeting in person. Now, there was already apprehension because we were bringing 141 principals to an in-person meeting during a pandemic, masked up and sitting about six feet apart in our boardroom.

I remember talking with Kelly, my coauthor and friend, the day before. We normally meet on Mondays and I shared how I wanted to continue being comfortable and began wearing my head wrapped. In addition, I wanted to wear one of the African print dresses that I had made. I was going back and forth trying to come up with every excuse in the book that this was a bad idea.

Kelly said, "What would happen if you did wear it? They cannot fire you for it. Wear it!"

I toiled with the idea throughout the night. The apprehension was real for me. Hundreds of what-ifs played in my head. After a night of toiling and fear of the known and unknown, I said, "Fuck it!" I walked up the thirty-six steps of the main building, head facing straight forward, hoping that my look was not that noticeable. Almost instantly, the receptionist recognized me and said, "Girl, I really like that head wrap. Where did you get it from?" A smile crept across my face. As more people were arriving for the meeting, I received so many compliments from women and unspoken words from Black women who smiled widely and gave me the sista' head nod. It was an empowering moment for me to shed one of my layers and be more of who I am. Sisters still talk with me about my newfound look and my courage to wear my hair wrapped and dress in an Afrocentric style.

This may seem like an inconsequential story to some, but for me, this is where my authenticity begins—shedding some layers to reveal who the real me is, becoming uncaged, untamed, unwrapped, and living into my truth. So when Glennon Doyle says, "We were taught to believe that who we are in our natural state is bad and dangerous," the deep scars of this perceived danger led me to question myself and my worth. Now, layer race, and then you have a cocktail of gender oppression and racial caging. These perceptions and the fear associated with them became my reality. I leaned into them and carried them like prized possessions. In some cases, I taught them by modeling and coaching. The emotional draining was the internal reckoning needed to help me to reveal my truth. Sometimes in the actual moment of reckoning, you cannot see the blessing. You are clouded by hurt that we do not lean into the hurt and leverage it to peel the layers and open up to the real.

Self-Awareness

Now, this shedding peels off like a Band-Aid on a healing scar. You know that the Band-Aid needs to come off. You anticipate that it will hurt and you hesitate to pull at it. You would rather keep it on rather than reveal what's underneath. So, you pull it slowly, biting your lip in pain and stopping intermittently to gather more nerve to continue pulling until finally, you yank. Ouch! And just like that, it's over and the air on the scar is inviting and refreshing.

As humans, we are born with a sixth sense, an internal gut check. This sense helps us to know when there is danger or something off-kilter:

"Don't walk down that dark alley."

"Maybe you should not take that way to work this morning."

"It may not be a good idea to send that email."

These warning signs help us to avoid physical, emotional, and psychological danger. As protection, we "put on armor" to help keep us safe and well. The armor is necessary when there is danger but at times it can become part of our permanent wardrobe, prohibiting us from being vulnerable, sharing our true selves, and being our authentic selves. In *Daring Greatly*, Brené Brown says, "Whether we're fourteen or fifty-four, our armor and our masks are as individualized and unique as the personal vulnerability, discomfort, and pain we're trying to minimize." Brown continues, "I was surprised to discover that we all share a small array of common protection mechanisms...I hope that a peek inside the armory will help us to look inside ourselves. How do we protect ourselves? When and how did we start using these defense mechanisms? What would it take to make us put the armor away?"[19]

---

19   Brené Brown. *Daring Greatly: How the Courage to Be Vulnerable Transforms the Way We Live, Love, Parent, and Lead.* (New York: Avery, 2015.) pps. 114-115.

Peeking inside also means declaring that I am enough. Now, what would that take? I am reminded of the Broadway musical adaptation of Alice Walker's critically acclaimed novel *The Color Purple*. The transformation of Celie at the end of the play where she finally stands against Mister and declares, I am here! In this powerful anthem, Celie recounts all of the abuse she took from Mister—the separation from her sister, the sexual assault, the removal of her children, and the constant degradation, physical, and emotional abuse. At that moment, she sheds the armor and sings out that she has everything she needs inside of her to live a bountiful life. She is thankful for loving who she really is.

As part of my work developing leaders, I have had the privilege of learning the social psychology of the human condition—what makes us tick and how our personalities, talents, and behaviors develop our leadership acumen. I have participated in the DISC assessment, Myers-Briggs, Gallup CliftonStrengths®, Fierce Conversations, and the Effectiveness Institute's Behavior Styles Assessment, and I am a certified facilitator in most of them. I actively engaged in learning about myself and how to support others as they interrogate their ideas, action, and leadership moves. I was always reflective about my work and behavior. I continued to learn more about who I was and how and why I lead. I have read many self-discovery books and articles to help me be a better educator and leader.

And with all of the learning, I felt that something was missing. As I walked away from each training, workshop, or book study, there was always a similar lesson: "If you simply become more aware of yourself, engage in these tools, you can adjust, fit in, and find success." So, in essence, if I just work harder then I will be successful. I was following the advice and guidance but felt stuck. Not stuck about knowing how I operate but stuck with feeling like myself as I operated within my home and work environments. What I discovered is that these traits, styles, conversations, and talents were not absent from personal and professional contexts. These strategies and tools were made to fit in an American, White, patriarchal, capitalist structure. For example, my top-five CliftonStrengths® are Achiever®, Learner®, Relator®, Belief®, and Responsibility®. Now, these talent dimensions or strengths really describe how I show up at work and home.

When I took the assessment and read the description of my top-five strengths, I was not surprised by them. I "took" the assessment so the answers should reflect my input. What was interesting about the report was the accompanying action planning document that was used to help me invest in my talents to turn them into strengths. I thought of many different ways I could leverage my talents to support my colleagues and my work. I requested opportunities to develop professional learning for novices, embed equity into content, and design opportunities to coach and mentor leaders. Many times, I design or craft ideas well in advance for my colleagues and boss to respond to, but inevitably, decisions are made last-minute, causing frantic planning and delivery. You get the best of me when the purpose is clear, I have adequate time and resources, and I am executing at high levels.

Many of these talents are more pronounced than others, especially my Achiever® and Responsibility® talent. A lot of these were molded when I was a young girl as I observed my mother and grandmother support the household. I lean on these strengths at work and I recognize how these talents are the same attributes designated for high-potential and achieving employees, but these same talents are muted for women and people of color. My Achiever® strengths can be perceived by men or my White counterparts as dominating, overbearing, and aggressive. The "angry Black woman" stereotype steeps in like a tea bag in lukewarm water. As I jump in and give my energy to a project, my intentions, ideas, and drive are immediately questioned or "paused." The energy and passion are misread as cocky or bossy. At times, the ideas are co-opted and then used as original thoughts by someone else.

But my male counterparts are not questioned or told to halt in the same way I am. And some of my White female counterparts are given a bit more grace. Dang, you can't win for trying! It is an exhausting dance that we engage in as we try to hold our own and support the organizations in which we work. What I am learning is that these traits, profiles, and strengths are not neutral. They manifest differently based on race, gender, and ability. There are undercurrent lessons that women and people of color have to learn to survive. This awareness helps me navigate the spaces in a way that helps to protect my mind and spirit while giving and getting energy the best way I know how. Now, this is exhausting and requires a level of practice and skills taught from a very early age. These skills are modeled by other women and women of color who endure this double standard in the workplace and social settings. It is like a rite of passage we endure to become accomplished at living in two worlds. So, with this awareness, there are two things I can do:

1. continue living an exhausting life and navigating the space as best I can, or

2. recognize that this is not mentally sustainable and take a stand.

I choose the second option because I know it is right, and I am scared to death. This option has led to the creation of this book and the story that I am telling to give me the courage to move from simply surviving. Let me start by shedding what I have been wearing and letting you see all of me.

Who am I? I am five feet tall. I am scared of fog. I *love* Star Wars. I think I need to lose weight and want to have a tummy tuck to get rid of the mommy pouch. I have Barney Rubble feet. I am quite smart. I am quick-witted. I rarely cry outward but cry a lot on the inside. I cannot see myself without my husband. I need him in my life. My sons are my treasures. I love them so much. I chose the most fulfilling job as an educator. I love stability and long for spontaneity. I am scared to death of venturing to start my own business. I believe I am not good enough. I have doubts. I want to be braver. I wish I could sing. I occasionally sneak chocolate. I love to learn. I want to be a badass. I am a leader and sometimes I don't want to be. I want to live on the beach and sell ice cream. I have a vivid imagination. I hate numbers. I love teaching. I am my mother's child. I am a lot like her but won't admit it to her face. I am bold, and I occasionally, well more often than not, say what is in my head.

I am here!

This is the beginning of my liberation.

This is where I long to be and I am on the journey to get there.

Hustling

To be who I am requires hustle. Doing anything I need to get done to meet the objective. True hustlers do not waver. They go for it! They navigate, fall, get back up, and keep it moving. In my recovery, this is where I want to be.

Now, I have been "sort of hustling" throughout my life. There were periods of lucidity. I would be firing on all cylinders, being a problem solver, problem avoider, planner, and thinking about ways to improve the work and recognition of women, especially Black women. But then I would get knocked down and retreat into my comfort zone. Eventually, I would slowly make my way back to that space. I have a tattoo of a phoenix on my back. It is a reminder of the hustler I want to be. You see, it is in me. Subconsciously, I know.

There are two types of hustling, and I have engaged in them both. Pretending to be who I am is a way to con people into thinking that I am who I am. The one that I long to be is husting for myself—going through my life with a sense of awareness and purpose. This recent journey of recovery has led me to uncover my imposter hustling so that I can move more to purposeful hustling.

I met Jason when I was twelve years old. As I shared in my origin story, he was the bigheaded boy who lived across the street from me. Over the years, we formed a close relationship as friends. He would make me laugh, listen to my stories, and debate the complexities of relationships. As we went off to college we stayed in touch. While we had other relationships, we continued to go to the movies, dinner, and share more laughs. It was after college that our relationship changed. We saw each other differently. We were grown-up, mature, and knew what each of us wanted. We saw it in each other. We wanted each other. We dated for two years before we got married and our lives were full. We had so much fun! God blessed me with an example of love like no other. He was everything that I hoped for and learned about in a good man. My family adored him and looked at our relationship as a model. After we had children, we redirected much of our attention to them. It was important to us to show them a loving home and family, but I was losing myself. I was growing concerned about the what-ifs.

We were rearing two Black boys. I wanted to make sure they were safe. Oh, God! What if? The thought of the unknown for them haunted me and I thrust myself into control. I planned everything and worried about everything. On the outside, people admired me for being a strong, stern, well-planned parent. On the inside, I was keeping it together. My husband started to notice a change, but I played it off. Just tired. Just busy. Just eager. Just working hard. Just …

I went from lots of fun to very serious and focused. I hustled him, family, work, friends, and then some. It only went deeper as I continued to get praise for my relationships. What people did not know is that I was bearing the weight of having to conform to a life that I did not feel fit for me. I wore it snuggly but it began constricting me—taking my breath away. Now, the majority of it was good. I am not complaining. I am only trying to express the other layers that shaped how I began navigating my life differently when I became responsible for the lives of others while forgoing my own life.

This was paralleled in my work life, too. As an educator, I wanted to be a model for my students. Show them that if they work hard, they can be like me—educated, out of the "hood" or giving back to it, successful, and so on. I flaunted myself before them every day, telling them that they can do it—work harder, study more, be more serious, give it your all. If you do all these things, you will be accepted and successful. I missed the lesson. I missed what I was supposed to be teaching—to be you! Be the best version of yourself and not me. Love who you are and be confident in all of the strange, quirky, endearing, hard, soft, annoying, carefree, rigid, people you are.

Now that I have grown up in my leadership, motherhood, wifehood, sisterhood, friendship, and womanhood, I see that I was only layering my students, teachers, family, and friends in what I thought they should be and not supporting who they already are. Paulo Freire, *Pedagogy of the Oppressed*, states, "Education either functions as an instrument which is used to facilitate integration of the younger generation into the logic of the present system and bring about conformity or it becomes the practice of freedom, the means by which men and women deal critically and creatively with reality and discover how to participate in the transformation of their world."[20] This is where I begin to model. I am working on removing the layers I have been wearing for nearly fifty years. It is heavy and comfortable. As I remove each layer, I can breathe. My shoulders lift as I inhale and there is a bit more confidence in my stance. Not the one that is stubborn and rigid, but the one where I can smile with the delight that I am no longer in fear. This is the hustle.

Forgiveness and Truth

Much has been written about and taught to me about the power of forgiveness. My mother always taught my brother and me to forgive people. She told us that everyone has their own story. She also told us that the first person we need to forgive is ourselves. For many years, I have been carrying shame, guilt, regrets, and self-doubt. I tried my best to hide them for fear of appearing weak. Not owning these feelings and dealing with the moments of pain only layered more masks until I became unrecognizable to myself. So, let me begin by apologizing to myself. To Kendra, I seek your forgiveness and permission to be okay with the struggle and the unveiling. As I am seeking the truth for myself, I permit myself to remove the shame I have been carrying on the inside. I will reveal my inner thoughts as a way to make visible the scars.

To my husband and children, I will be a bit different than you have seen me. It will be a bit strange but I think you will like me better. I need your help as I wrestle through the real me. I am going to fall. I need your belief and strength to get me back up. to help me get back up.

To my former students, I am sorry for not being a better teacher, better leader, and better me. You had only parts of me and the best

---

20   Paulo Freire, *Pedagogy of the Oppressed* (New York: Penguin, 2017) p. 34

version of me I thought I should be. I promise to continue working on modeling authentic leadership. You deserve it.

To my sisters in leadership and especially in educational leadership. I know how hard you are working to prove yourself worthy of the awesome responsibility of creating the best learning environment for our students. I know the challenges you are navigating, in addition to the hard work of leading a school. I am sorry for not sharing my whole truth. Our community of leaders needs us, and I promise to share my new learning with you. You will see me more vulnerable than I have ever been, and I will not apologize for it.

You may be asking, *What impact will seeking forgiveness for myself and others have on my work as a leader?* This is leadership! Leadership is influence. The first person you have to lead is you. If you prioritize yourself, you will save yourself. As you navigate patriarchal and/or majority-White environments, you have to be comforted in your real self. And if your real self cannot thrive in the environment, you may have to make the space for yourself and others to be free and fiercely productive. I am on that journey.

Questions to ponder as you become unwrapped:

1. What are you carrying that you should shed?
2. Why are you carrying the extra weight? What happened in your life that required the extra baggage?
   a. Who are you?
   b. Who are you that people know?
   c. Who are you that people need to know?
   d. Who are you really?

3. Are you living your life as who you really are? If so, what does it feel like? If not, what do you need to do to live your life fully?

4. Who do you have in your life to check that you are being authentically you? What permission are you giving him/her/them to hold you able?

Strategies and tools you already know. Now use them with a different lens.

- Journal—write your thoughts on paper. Try to make sense of the conversation that is in your head.

- Read. Learn your history and interrogate what is being taught to you. Look for all sides of the story. Search for the story behind the story.

- Lean on your best friend. Not the best friend that will only stroke your ego, the other best friend that will tell you your shit does stink.

- Find a hobby or activity that feeds your mind, body, and soul.

- Take a risk and find your passion. This may mean creating your own space to thrive.

FROM ALLY TO COCONSPIRATOR

I am not free while any woman is unfree even when her shackles are very different from my own.

— AUDRE LORDE

I WAS ANXIOUS, nervous, and unsure of what to wear. I knew I wanted to show up authentically, but I did not know what people would think. If you had known me when I was a teenager and young adult, you would not think I would be afraid of what people would think if I showed up wearing an African print headwrap and a brightly colored dress to a leadership meeting. After a summer of shelter in place, financial uncertainty, and racial unrest, I wrestled with how to redirect my life in a way that resurrected me. For a few years, I had been lost. I had followed a specific formula:

> *Move out of the 'hood, get a good education and job, keep busy, sprinkle in a family, balance both, and—voila—success! The world will be your oyster.*

Now, don't get me wrong. I am blessed with the life I have. I love my work. I have a loving family. And I live comfortably—but something was off. I did not feel like I was me. It was as if I was an imposter in my own skin. It came to a head last summer with the racial reckoning we have not seen in this country since the 1950s. The killing of Breonna Taylor, Ahmaud Arbery, and the eight minutes and forty-five seconds of life snuffed from George Floyd jolted me back to life, Black life. As a mother of two Black sons, rage and fear burned inside me. I began to question what I had been doing in my life. For forty-nine years, I had tried to be accepted, learn the ways to "fit in." At what cost? I was still navigating the between—good enough to be accepted and not good enough to sell out. And, as a Black female, the dynamics are twofold. The ladder to climb is steep and long, with barbed wire, deteriorated rungs, and a ceiling at the top. I have seen highly educated, polite, well-dressed Black women—the approved model of the American way—be ostracized by White women for being too pretty and ambitious, by White men for being too bossy and over-reaching, and by Black men and women for acting too White or not being Black enough. I was exhausted! So, I was done! I had to focus on myself.

So, when I decided to strip some of the layers of "pretend me" on that September day, I struggled. It was like trying to break a very bad habit. The detoxing sent chills through my body. I had a nervous flutter in my belly. I was sweating and pacing. I cannot believe it was so hard to decide if I should wear a head wrap to work. Kelly and I had our scheduled weekly call to discuss women in leadership when I shared my conundrum. She looked at me with an awkward stare, tilting her head slightly. I paused because I was taken aback by her expression.

"Kendra, is there anything in the policy that says that you cannot wear your head wrap?"

"No," I said, sheepishly.

"So, wear it!"

Wear it! The audacity of her to declare that I could simply do this. Now, Kelly, a White woman, did not have to think twice about this decision. She noted the non-existence of a policy and simply exclaimed, do it! This is where our relationship turned. She paused as I looked away from the camera, and her tone changed. She went from telling and giving advice to listening.

"Kelly, it is not that simple, and yet it is." I began to tell her the stories of the "lessons" I was taught when I started my job. If I wanted to fit it, I needed to dress like this, talk like that, wear my hair like this—and, God forbid, do not show my tattoos. I had to navigate being female and Black which meant not making others around me, particularly my White counterparts, feel uncomfortable. When Kelly said, "Wear it," I knew at that moment I did not have all of the privileges to simply do it. And, at that moment, she recognized it. She recognized me.

We talked for about an hour, unpacking this seemingly bold move on my part, sharing additional stories of the intersectionality of race and gender. Kelly listened. I talked. In the end, I told her I would continue to think about what to wear and decide in the morning.

Kendra, it's just a headwrap! was the White woman privileged thinking that initially came to mind. *What's the big deal?* was my first reaction. *If there isn't a policy, then you are clear to wear what you want,* said my White experience. My lack of understanding of her struggle was filtered through a lens of never having to be concerned about how to speak, what to wear, the acceptability of my hair style, and how to control my emotions and reactions. Those were unrelatable matters in my White paradigm.

Don't get me wrong, I have too many misogynistic experiences that I allowed to dictate how I showed up as a woman. White people have our own trauma from White supremacy culture to unpack and heal from. But those experiences are very different from the ones that have put my friend in the position to question whether or not she should wear her head wrap. The basis of those experiences however, did not include the color of my skin. I saw the reaction on my friend's face. One of bewilderment and inquisition at the same time.

"It's not that easy, you see."

And in those words, I knew it was time to listen to my dear friend tell her story, offload her fear, and share with me her experience as a Black woman in a position of leadership in a Southern school district. And so, we began. We began to hold that brave and sacred space for one another. I learned what she needed most from me was to be heard and seen in the same way I wanted—and want to—be heard and seen. I knew then I needed to be more than her friend or ally.

Her story of being told how to show up, the southern "bless your heart" experiences she'd had over and over as a Black woman who'd grown up in Harlem, began her career in the Bronx, and was laboring to be successful in the South were my lessons to learn. All the while I listened, I thought, *How do I move from allyship to accomplice and ultimately coconspirator? How will I risk my own White privilege in her name so she can be seen and heard? How will we as women begin to show up as a collective and create new cultures and systems where we can thrive?*

And with the story of the headwrap, we began to envision and cocreate together a new workplace where women, all women, can show up and be seen. We talked about how the well-being of women in school leadership suffers and no one talks about it, about how scarcity (not feeling like we are enough) holds us back from taking risks and going after that which we most desire and makes us feel fully human. How not speaking up when we so deeply want to is a cause of immense frustration, resentment, and shame is not benign. And how we were not taught the words to use to create our own boundaries.

Sonya Renee Taylor tells us in her quote about returning to life after the pandemic "We are given an opportunity to stitch a new garment. One that fits all of humanity and nature."[21] How do we stitch a new garment, like the headwrap, that fits all women who want to live and lead in their full humanity? We share so many of the same experiences at work as women trying to rise from the river in cultures that continually throw us back in. We are forced to segment ourselves to be accepted when what we really want is to integrate every part of who we are into our work and to belong.

Kendra and I share a fundamental belief that if we want to see more women rise to senior-level positions in education and remain in those positions, we must go beyond mentoring and networking. Mentoring and networking are necessary but not sufficient. We need new skill sets, a new way to practice our way of leadership, a keen understanding of our strengths so we can show up authentically and not hustle, words that allow us to create healthy boundaries, governing bodies that understand women can lead differently and achieve similar, if not, greater results, and accomplices and coconspirators who are willing to risk their privilege to allow others to soar. We must intentionally know and own our stories to unwrap the social conditioning that we all experience as young girls growing up with gender expectations and write a new bold, courageous, vulnerable ending for ourselves and other women.

---

21   Sonya Renee Taylor, April 2, 2020, https://www.instagram.com/p/B-fc3ejAlvd/?

~

So, here is the rest of the story.

The next day, I wore it! I remember walking up the thirty-six steps of my office building and taking a deep breath as I opened the main door.

"Wow, I love your head wrap," exclaimed the receptionist at the desk.

Okay, that was one comment. I dropped off my belongings and headed to the hallway to greet the leaders entering the building. This was it. The moment of truth. As they began filtering in, I noticed the pleasant surprise in the eyes of my sisters and brothers. My sisters air-hugged me and/or gave the Black girl's nod of approval. My brothers gave a thumbs-up. My White colleagues openly stated how beautiful my wrap and dress were. Exhale! Others either did not openly acknowledge the difference in my dress or refused to comment. Either way, I held my head high that day and smiled under my matching mask. I took pictures that morning and sent them to Kelly.

"You look gorgeous!"

That sealed the deal for our relationship. We vowed to support each other and all women by listening to their stories, educating ourselves—doing the work to understand, speak up, and defend our sisters. We love each other. We are allies and working toward being coconspirators.

So, here we are, at the crossroads of the book, sharing how our paths crossed in ways we did not foresee. We knew each other for thirteen years before this moment. Thirteen! This is our lucky number. This moment collided with our worlds. This was our intersection in space and in time. You never know how, where, and when people will come into your life and have a profound impact on your self-discovery and recovery. A wrap is more than a symbolic headpiece to signify importance and visibility. It is also a statement. It's a wrap!

It is the end of our guarded talks, our "safe" speech, our comfortable lives. These days are over. We will model the vulnerability needed to understand our perspectives. We will honor and recognize that differences are assets, not deficiencies. We start with ourselves. We meet weekly to discuss what we are reading, what we are learning, and to have a knee-slapping belly laugh. We talk about our lived experiences and welcome each other in our personal family spaces. Kelly had the opportunity to meet with my family on our weekly family Zoom check-in. I recall how nervous I was for her to meet my family because the matriarchs of the family were ready! Even though we were on Zoom, it was like we were in person with ten sets of eyes small and staring, trying to figure her out.

"What does she do?"

"What does she really want to learn about us?"

"What does this White lady want to know about us?"

The guard was up, and I knew how they felt. Five of my cousins lived through the Civil Rights era, and now they were living through another American racial reckoning. I wanted them to know the woman I have come to respect and love as a colleague and friend. A woman who was walking alongside me to learn how we face a racialized, patriarchal society as women and educational leaders.

Kelly and I planned for the meeting, and I could tell she was nervous, too. She wanted to facilitate a discussion with my family about their values and the connection with food. Kelly is a great listener. Because of all of the stories I have shared with her over the years about my family's closeness through food, Kelly was intrigued by our family bond and how food was the anchor for each story.

I spoke about our packed apartment with cousins, aunts, grand-parents, great aunts, "friend cousins," and close and distant family members who would play cards, drink, and eat.

These weekend gatherings were a staple in my family. This is where I learned the stories of the South and the food they'd make like red rice, chitterlings, mash, macaroni and cheese, greens, pig feet, fried fish, cornbread, black-eyed peas, and my cousin's famous coleslaw. And with each story about food was a lesson I learned about how to survive, from how to hold the house keys in my hand as a weapon to how to sit like a lady and fight like a man. All of these lessons are part of me—part of my sweetness and my fight.

Kelly and I talked about a way to get my family to speak about these lessons and cuisine. She designed a PowerPoint presentation to get the family to speak about how and why this connection is critical to our family culture. The slides were beautiful. She had captured the essence of our family, but I had to break it to her.

"Cut out some of these slides. They will not be engaged in the way you are thinking."

You see, my family is not going to sit through a "presentation." That is not who they are. The casual, off-the-cuff conversation is what moves them. Anything that smells like or looks like an inter-vention, an interrogation, and/or the "none of your business" talk throws them in a tizzy, and it will be talked about for months and maybe years. As much as she was preparing for them, I was prepar-ing them for her. And I was close to successful.

The virtual meeting started okay, with family and friends intro-ducing themselves and sharing what they value about the family. There were a few jokes and smiles. My nerves calmed as they seemed to be engaged in the conversation. But then, Cousin Brenda led with one snide remark and the meeting went there. She was a bit tipsy, so the comment was both exaggerated and factual. "I know you don't know some of what we are talking about, right? Because you are White."

Well, that was the start of the end. My brother let in next. He wanted to make sure that Kelly knew that our partnership was just that—a partnership. He warned that the font on the book needed to be equal. Oh shit! Now they were on a roll. I looked at Kelly. She held her own. Listened and nodded that she understood. My mom echoed the comment but then put everything in perspective about using her privilege to support me and make a difference.

After Kelly shared that her home was approximately one mile from a sacred Black burial ground, the conversation turned again. Momma Karen, as she is affectionately called in the urban farming world, lowered her head, shifted in her chair, and proceeded with her history lesson. She encouraged Kelly to look into ways to honor the Blacks that were buried there. Thank God for the Soul of America, which was scheduled to begin on CNN at 9:30 p.m., or I don't want to imagine what would have happened next.

Why do I tell this story? Because Kelly listened. Again, she listened and used the moment to try to learn and understand how and why my family was concerned about her motives. These feelings are deeply rooted in race, White power, and White privilege. They wanted to make sure that the power was not tipped. Thanks, fam, and thanks Kelly for being in the moment.

I do not possess intuitive allyship superpowers. That is to say, I did not arrive at an understanding of how first to listen to Kendra and her long-held desire to show up at work authentically as herself. I did not naturally grasp the understanding that, when her family questioned me, they wanted to understand my willingness to risk and lay down my privilege in the name of justice and equity for their sister, daughter, niece, and cousin. I had to do my own work first to have a full understanding of what it meant and the courage to show up as an ally. I had to learn to be vulnerable and able to sit in uncertainty and risk being a coconspirator for and with my friend. I needed to understand that systems were built on patriarchy and White supremacy, that my privilege exists simply and not so simply based on the color of my skin, and I needed to learn the history of our country I was never taught.

In exploring my origin story, I discovered how I was conditioned to move through this world. I was the peacekeeper and symbolic giver of gifts for others. I needed to do my own personal independent work first so I could garner the skill sets and words I needed to show up confidently and fearlessly for myself. We, White women, have work to do. Work to understand the social conditioning that keeps us from being who we want to be and how we have been complicit in creating conditions that silence women who have been historically marginalized. We start by developing a greater sense of self so we can share power with other women, be audaciously brave, and say no to those who ask us to uphold the status quo. We need to check our hubris and gather our humility by taking a back seat, allowing others to lead, and be seen.

By exploring our stories, understanding what's preventing us from showing up for ourselves, and developing the skills to engage in complicated and uncomfortable conversations, we can move to true allyship and aspire to become coconspirators. This will be our way forward and how we create the conditions where all women can thrive and belong. Whoopie Goldberg once said, "We are here for a reason. I believe a bit of the reason is to throw little torches out to lead people through the dark." It's time we throw little torches and begin to lead each other out of the dark.

Dr. Bettina Love, author of *We Want To Do More Than Survive*, talks and teaches us about allies, accomplices, and coconspirators. In her interview at Columbia University Teachers College, she is asked to describe the difference between these three stages. She explains that an ally is a cheerleader, someone who knows all the "language," reads the books, and knows all the right things to say. An ally is someone who is doing her work, listening, and not just reading all the books but using them to transform herself. It's the first step we must take for ourselves as women leaders and the first step we must take to amplify the voices of so many women who have been sidelined for too long. The essential behavior to being a true ally and preparing yourself for what comes next is listening. Truly listening. Not the kind of listening we do when we are simply waiting to respond. But listening to understand.

Dr. Love goes on to explain the purpose of allyship is to prepare ourselves for the next level in becoming an accomplice. An accomplice is willing to act when the situation presents itself. It might be in a meeting when we first become our own accomplice and speak our truth and show up authentically. Or, when we have an opportunity to speak up for another woman whose voice has been drowned out.

And finally, our journey leads us to become coconspirators. In becoming a coconspirator, you are the sum of all your work and you create opportunities to disrupt systems. You don't just wait for them. We create those opportunities by asking for what we want and need and speaking up when an injustice of any level occurs. We are coconspirators when White women are willing to put their White privilege on the line and take a risk on behalf of other women who do not possess the same entitlements simply based on how they look. We come to this work in trust, love, commitment to disrupt, and create opportunities for all.

When we examine the work of the abolitionist, as Dr. Love teaches, we see coconspirators. The Underground Railroad would not have been possible without those who were willing to risk their privilege to break the system of oppression. This is our work together. I am a White woman. I have privilege because of the color of my skin. I did nothing to earn it. It just is. I have and will always continue to do my work of listening and learning. I pledge to show up as an accomplice when the opportunity is presented to me. And I commit myself to the work of being a coconspirator for myself, for Kendra, and for all other women leaders who deserve to work and lead in systems that recognize their full humanity.

Our work is complex. Trying to boil it down to simple lessons and answers is the wrong move. That is why it is important to use the appropriate language to call out the issues of gender and race with the appropriate terminology. For example, it is important to discuss structural racism, sexism, gendered racism, intersectionality, feminism, patriarchy, oppression, micro and macro aggressions, discrimination, and stereotyping.

For the purposes of this book and lessons, we underscore sexism, patriarchy, and gendered racism.

Sexism

According to the Global Citizen, sexism is "any act, gesture, visual representation, spoken or written words, practice, or behavior based upon the idea that a person or a group of persons is inferior because of their sex, which occurs in the public or private sphere, whether online or offline."[22] We use this definition because it is a globally agreed-upon definition where the structures, processes, and practices that lead to discrimination against women are rooted in the historically unequal power relations between men and women—which leads to discrimination and prevents the full advancement of women in *society*. It is rare to find a woman in any line of work or profession who hasn't experienced acts of misogyny or sexism.

When I was in college and worked at the campus cafeteria, I experienced unwanted advances every day I showed up at work. The cafeteria manager made verbal assaults and snide remarks about the way I was dressed. He habitually asked what I was doing after work. Not out of interest but out of an uncomfortable curiosity. It was always the same. I laughed it off to keep my job and the peace. I didn't have the words to tell him what I really thought about his unwanted advances. I could not muster the courage or words to tell him how I felt about his behavior or to demand he stop. My conditioning, lack of much-needed skills, words, and understanding of what I was experiencing, and my fear kept me silent.

We often tell women to "grow a backbone." Our backbones are strong because we have been carrying the weight of society for centuries, especially Black and Brown women. We don't need stronger backbones. We need to unwrap the way we have been conditioned, and we need each other. This, unfortunately, would not be the last time I experienced this kind of misogynistic behavior from a male supervisor or colleague. What I always marvel at was how they delivered their words with such bravado and without fear of reprisal.

---

22   Imogen Calderwood and Erica Sánchez, "There's Finally an Internationally Agreed upon Definition of Sexism. Here's Why That Matters.," Global Citizen, April 2019, https://www.globalcitizen.org/en/content/sexism-definition-council-of-europe-equality/#:~:text=Sexism%20is%20defined%20as%3A%20%E2%80%9CAny,%2C%20whether%20online%20or%20offline.%E2%80%9D

Over time, I have worked to understand my own unique strengths, undo many of the ways I have been taught to show up in the world, gain skills, increase my knowledge, and most of all, use words in order to ask for what I want and need, as well as to change systems and cultures—not just for myself, but for all women. Maya Angelou teaches us, "Each time a woman stands up for herself, without knowing it possibly, without claiming it, she stands up for all women."

Patriarchy

Patriarchy is "a form of social, economic and political structuring of society produced by the gradual relations created and reinforced by different institutions linked closely to achieve consensus on the lesser value of women roles."[23] According to the feminist view of patriarchy, Gerda Lerner states that patriarchy is a "human invention" that was appropriate for a time but then it was institutionalized and normalized, creating the oppressive practices we see today. When we can have a president elected who has had numerous affairs and openly states that he can assault women, then what message are we sending to men and women about power?

In the now-infamous Access Hollywood interview, Donald Trump describes his "sexual advances" toward married women. "I don't even wait. And when you're a star, they let you do it. You can do anything. Grab 'em by the pussy. You can do anything." And, he was able to do anything! Men and women continued to rally around him and disregard his repeated sexist remarks. So how does this seep into the conditioning in our schools which serve as a microcosm of

---

23   Alda Facio, "What Is Patriarchy? - Learnwhr.org" (Women's Human Rights Institute, 2013), http://www.learnwhr.org/wp-content/uploads/D-Facio-What-is-Patriarchy.pdf.

our society? You see it play out in the dress codes, athletics, course loads, and teacher and leadership positions.

When we examine the history of education and schooling, we learn that initially teaching and leading in schools was considered "women's work." Women were considered better nurturers of children. It was in their nature. This was not a strength or talent to be developed but rather it was looked upon as our innate way of being. Educating and leading schools were also left to women as it allowed local governing bodies and school boards to keep pay low and benefits few. Over time, the practice of school leadership became more "professional," an increase in credentialing and qualifications was required, and the perception grew that leading a school or district was honorable.

As this occurred, those jobs tended to go to men. The use of the GI bill to obtain graduate degrees and the advent of school-level athletic coaching were actions and steps that led to more men being selected as principals and superintendents.[24] As women continued to enter the profession as teachers, the systems and cultures that led to advancement were being created and built by men. This created the norms around what "best practice" looked like for a principal and superintendent. The few women who were elevated into those positions were expected to perform just like their male predecessors and to obey the system. And, thus, a prototype of the senior-level school leader was created. Women have since worked to conform to that prototype. This is the genesis of the patriarchal system we must begin to disrupt.

---

24   Robert Maranto et al., "Boys Will Be Superintendents: School Leadership as a Gendered Profession," kappanonline.org, October 3, 2018, https://kappanonline.org/maranto-carroll-cheng-teodoro-school-leadership-gender/.

Gendered Racism

Gendered racism is the intersection of gender and racism. Kimberle Crenshaw, noted law professor, researcher, author, and speaker, recently redefined intersectionality as "a lens, a prism, for seeing the way in which various forms of inequality often operate together and exacerbate each other." In her 1989 article, "Demarginalizing the Intersection of Race and Sex: A Black Feminist Critique of Antidiscrimination Doctrine, Feminist Theory and Antiracist Politics," intersectionality was a term used to "describe how race, class, gender, and other individual characteristics 'intersect' with one another and overlap."[25]

Today, the term is under attack by conservative White folx, who believe that this proposes a threat to the American way—attributing to the theory or idea of victim shaming and White blaming. Dr. Crenshaw introduced the term as a rebuttal to legal decisions facing discrimination cases against women of color. She argues that you cannot simply rule for or against discriminatory practices without taking into consideration the multiple identities and the intersection of gender and race.

For example, Dr. Crenshaw illustrates how the courts frame the stories of Black women. She further explains that the courts cited that "Black women" are not a protected class, therefore they could not rule against discrimination. Dr. Crenshaw argues that race and gender are a protected class and failure to see these two as intersected is the failure to support and protect Black women from mistreatment and discrimination in the workforce. In fact, in the *DeGraffenreid v. General Motors* ruling, the court stated: "this lawsuit must be examined to see if it states a cause of action

25   Kimberle Crenshaw, "Demarginalizing the Intersection of Race and Sex: A Black Feminist Critique of Antidiscrimination Doctrine, Feminist Theory and Antiracist Politics" (University of Chicago Legal Forum, 1989).

for race discrimination, sex discrimination, or alternatively either, but not a combination of both."[26] Intersectionality purports that a person's identity and experiences are not compartmentalized, but compounded lived experiences based on race and gender. These two cannot be isolated for they exist simultaneously. Dr. Crenshaw concluded that the "failure to embrace the complexities of compoundedness is not simply a matter of political will, but is also due to the influence of a way of thinking about discrimination which structures politics so that struggles are categorized as singular issues. Moreover, this structure imports a descriptive and normative view of society that reinforces the status quo."[27] So, what does it mean for women in educational leadership? This means that as we navigate the field of education, we must be aware of the intersection of lived experiences that guide our leadership as well as how we support and guide each other.

In Dr. Ibram X. Kendi's award-winning book, *How to Be an Antiracist,* he defined gendered racism as a powerful collection of racist policies that lead to inequity between race-genders and are substantiated by racist ideas about race-genders.[28] Dr. Kendi's description of gender racism is relayed in the story of his sexist and homophonic reckoning as he references Philomena Essed and Dr. Kimberle Crenshaw's work on feminism and intersectionality. Dr. Kendi is critical of the civil rights movement and the Black political movement for the treatment and the dismissal of Black women. Dr. Kendi states that "to truly be feminist is to be anti-

---

26   "DeGraffenreid v. General Motors Assembly Div., Etc., 413 F. Supp. 142 (E.D. Mo. 1976)," Justia Law, accessed January 29, 2022, https://law.justia.com/cases/federal/district-courts/FSupp/413/142/1660699/.

27   Kimberle Crenshaw, "Demarginalizing the Intersection of Race and Sex: A Black Feminist Critique of Antidiscrimination Doctrine, Feminist Theory and Antiracist Politics" (University of Chicago Legal Forum, 1989).

28   Ibram X. Kendi, *How to Be an Antiracist* (New York: One World, 2019). p. 181

racist. To be antiracist is to level the different race-genders, is to root the inequities between the equal race-genders in the policies of gender racism."[29]

In his most recent book, *Four Hundred Souls*, coedited with Dr. Keisha Blain, the chapter on Anita Hill, written by Salamisha Tillet, underscores the immense silencing and dismissal of the Black female story of oppression and sexism. Tillet's account of her recollection of the case is similar to mine. I was a sophomore at the University of Notre Dame at the start of the testimony. I remember seeing Anita Hill raise her right hand to solemnly swear to tell the truth and the immense grilling by the all-White male senators whose eyes fixed in disgust at her audacity to defend herself. They extolled her as an oversexualized opportunist while not giving any credence to Clarence Thomas's alleged harassment of her and other alleged women. And to top it off, Thomas called the hearing a "high-tech lynching." He used the most extreme analogy to gain favor among his White constituents.

I remember the pain in the pit of my stomach after hearing that. A lynching? Those words were used as a defense of his appalling behavior and harassment. He knew how it would land on his White counterparts, and Anita Hill could not come back from that. Black man, Clarence Thomas, gained White conservative male allies and assaulted her again, this time in court and the court of public opinion. I know that feeling. No one believes you. No one sees you as you are. It is like being in a crowded room, screaming at the top of your lungs, and no one can hear or see you. You are invisible in the din.

For women of color, intersectionality can make you feel invisible, voiceless. But what Anita Hill did was set a course for Black women to speak. As we watched her courage, we found ours. As

---

29   Ibid. p. 189

they attempted to strip her dignity, we regained ours. In fact, in November of 1991, the *New York Times* printed a full-page ad with the proclamation, "African American Women in Defense of Ourselves."[30] [31] There, sixteen hundred African American women submitted their names in support of Anita Hill and others who are victims of racial and sexual harassment and discrimination. Her courage is our courage. Her fight is our fight. Leadership is courage and sometimes the results of that courage include pain, sacrifice, and "firsts." *Firsts* speak out, speak up, and pave the way for others to be freer.

These terms are critical to understanding our work in women's education leadership, especially as our educational systems are critical to shaping the lives of the children in our care. At school, students learn to socialize in an empowered White male structure. Learning these terms will help us to become aware of how we learn and navigate the spaces. The awareness is how we begin to uncover our unintentional and intentional complicit behavior in the system so that we can begin to dismantle the frame in which we progress and lead. We share how we will do our work to improve learning and support each other.

Analyze the Space You Occupy

Kendra

To become antiracist and antisexist means to understand the space you occupy. While my upbringing as a Black woman led to my relative success in educational leadership despite challenging situ-

30   Rosemary Bray, "Taking Sides Against Ourselves," *The New York Times*, November 17, 1991.

31   "The Proclamation," Sisters Testify, accessed March 3, 2022, https://www.sisterstestify.com/about/the-proclamation/.

ations and environments, I am aware that as I have navigated the systems and structures, I have gained privilege. I am an educated middle-class woman who lives in the suburbs. This is very different from how I grew up and how I have taught and led the students within my school. This also means that my frame, context, and values drive my decisions. There are times when I have had to back up because I made White-lens assumptions about marginalized people and even perpetuated them in my teaching and leading. From the naming of my homerooms as a principal to the field trips that I would encourage my teachers to take, I looked at the pinnacle of success from a White lens and inadvertently shared that message with my students. It was not until I had my own reawakening, learning, and life experiences that I became cognizant of my lens.

The rudest awakening came when I took a course through Harvard's School of Education on Leadership Excellence and Equity, and I completed one of the antibias surveys. This is the one where you are looking at words and images of White and Black faces and making selections on the keyboard to determine "good," "bad" "safe" "smart," etc. So, when I took it the first time, I really concentrated on my typing, making sure I was quick enough with the keystrokes. My husband always says I do not know my right from my left. When I got the initial results, I blamed it on my directional ineffectiveness. I shrugged it off and prepared to take it again after now understanding the rules.

After the second time, I blamed it on stress and distractions at work. My mind was not right. I needed to do it at home with minimal interruptions. The third time, same results. Now, in writing this book, I see it. I see what I have been doing throughout my life. That is why I am in recovery and rediscovery. I did what I thought was right. I played the game, and in the end, I didn't win.

I am not meant to win. The game was not built for me. So, what do I do now that I know this? I have to re-examine my space again. This time, I have opened my eyes. When you know better, you do better and be better.

First, I want to apologize to all of my students to whom I have given parts of an education. An effective educational leader creates a school where students are free to advocate, question, and critically think about what and how they are learning. But as you think about how schools are designed, students are fed content, told to regurgitate it, and told to step back in line if they question what they are learning. Educators wield power, influence, and control, and students are impressionable. My conditioning followed the formula. You deserved more from me, and I promise to do better going forward with every opportunity I have to make a difference in the lives of students. As an education leader, I have to lead myself first and this means understanding fundamentally who I am.

This journey has been fraught with joy, disappointment, anger, embarrassment, and courage. I embrace it all! Real leadership starts with admitting your mistakes and learning from them. This is the environment I want students to experience. A learning space where they explore who they are and how they contribute to the world as an individual and as a group.

Second, I will read more and learn more. I will embark on my own reeducation so that I can show up authentically and help people to do the same. Lastly, I will always start my work by honoring people's experiences, the ancestors who have paved the way before me, and thank my colleagues for the opportunity and privilege to share my experiences.

Kelly

White women are battling against the patriarchy. Black, Indigenous, Women of Color fight against not just the patriarchy, but also stereotypes and a fabricated standard of what it means to be a woman in leadership. One of the lessons I took away from the conversation I had with Kendra concerning her desire to wear her headwrap was that it was not really about the headwrap. Rather, it was about her desire to show up authentically as herself. To be able to make her own choices, be they big or small. That included wearing what she wanted to wear on her head, how she wanted to dress, and choosing a hairstyle she wanted for herself. She wanted to shed the uniform of the black, gray, or blue suit that purposely was designed to make her invisible. Rather, she desired to wear bold, vibrant-colored clothing that was a symbol of her true self.

As I reflected on our conversation, I became stricken with sadness for her and for me. I have known Kendra for thirteen years, and we met shortly after she arrived in Gwinnett. All that time, I saw the same Kendra, looking like and dressing in a manner that suited the expected standard. I was distressed that all this time she'd had to hide a part of herself. I was also troubled and angry about not being able to experience all that vibrant, bold, gregarious Black woman had to offer. These are moments and experiences stolen from all of us, and the system was designed that way.

I pondered, *How do we begin to break down the stereotypes created about all women of color when systems are not safe for them to show up in all their full humanity? And how do White women experience all of what other women have to offer if it is not safe to do so?* It feels like being on a merry-go-round, circling around, going nowhere—and in the pursuit of "fitting in" rather than belonging.

As I began to do my own antiracism work with a keen interest in the intersection of race and gender, I began to understand that until we tear down and rebuild systems where all women can fully show up as who we are, and we experience each other in all that fullness, we will continue to hold the stereotypes of one another and assume our life experiences do not matter. Through my friendship and talks with Kendra and leading Black women through courageous leadership development, I am conscious of how lived experiences matter. When I first taught strengths understanding through coaching or facilitation, I believed all one needed to do was understand her strengths and apply them out in the world. When I taught courage-building skills, I believed all one needed to do was be more vulnerable, understand her values, create, and brave trust, and know how to rise again after a disappointment. I took the Nike approach to leadership and personal development—*just do it*. It's not that simple, and it's not that easy. Context and life experiences matter. Asking women, any and all women, to be more vulnerable matters in the context of the systems and cultures we navigate.

Seek Other Points of View

Kendra

Become a learner of people. Winston Churchill once said, "Courage is what it takes to stand up and speak. It is also what it takes to sit down and listen." This is one of the hardest things to do because our ego drives us to think we know it all and know what is right. This is a significant leadership move. As I seek to learn from others, I am learning their contexts and frames by which they see the world. This leads to fruitful and fierce conversation.

As Susan Scott states, a fierce conversation is where you "come from behind yourself and make it real."[32] That is what we are aiming for here. Real conversations. Ones where you listen to each other's perspectives, engage in meaningful debate, and come out of the conversation enriched. You know when you have had one of these conversations because your heart feels full, and you leave the conversation renewed. You have to open yourself up to this kind of listening and speaking. It seems like this may be a monumental task considering the current political divide, racial unrest, and aftermath of the COVID-19 pandemic, but this is the type of communication that we need to heal.

Bernadette and I met in 1994 when I was a first-year teacher in the West Farms section of the Bronx. I was a spirited twenty-one-year-old teacher who was ready to change the world. Teach for America has a way of sparking a particular type of energy from its corps members. The "save the world" mentality was in full effect.

But Bernie was the opposite. She was serious and socially cautious with me at first. I recall when the assistant principal came to my classroom to introduce Ms. Payne. She was going to be my paraprofessional. I did not even know what that was. My assistant? My co-teacher? A teacher monitor? I was happy to have the help and I welcomed her warmly. She did not reciprocate. I could tell that she did not want to be there. She stayed near the back of the classroom and watched my every move, not saying a word. This lasted for several days until she leaned in to make sure that students were staying on task. Her voice, smooth with a slight accent, startled me. After a while, she warmed up and attended to the most challenging students, getting them to complete assignments, engaging in class discussions, and keeping them on task. She emitted an aura

---

32   Susan Scott, *Fierce Conversations: Achieving Success at Work and in Life, One Conversation at a Time* (London, UK: Piatkus, 2017). p. 67.

that said, "Not today!" We often teased that she was her moniker—Ms. Pain. People just didn't mess with her.

Over the years, we became the best of friends. I am not sure what changed from our initial meeting, but when you saw me, you saw Ms. Payne. We each cared deeply about our work and our students. Bernie, as she is affectionately called, was strong, fearless, and driven. She made her own way. As a paraprofessional, Bernie was highly respected and respectfully feared. Kids loved her even when she seemed to dismiss them. She was like that tough-love mother with a hard exterior and soft heart. She loved her students and fought with and for them. Kids under her care flourished, fought for her, and fought for themselves.

In 2002, we had the opportunity to open a new middle school in the Bronx. I was a teacher and assistant director of the school, and Bernie was selected to be the dean of students. She had a way with them. Dean Payne talked straight with kids. She never softened, and that is why students loved her, and that is why I love her. She is one of the few people I call who will tell me the truth! She has seen me in my successes and my failures. She has watched me grow in my leadership and falter. All the while, she was open and honest with me. Bernie is a leader.

When I told her that I was writing a book for women leaders, she told me that she is a "fucking woman leader and empowered, shit!" That is Bernie! So, when I was in my moment of failure as a middle school principal, she did not try to appease my ego. She simply said, "You tried. You did some dumb shit, but you learn."

I could only chuckle. While I was looking for sympathy or someone to stroke my ego, she told me what I needed to hear. She reminded me that I am flawed. It is okay to own it and learn from it. Bernie is one of the wisest people I know. I always tried to encourage her to become a teacher and administrator. She has scoffed at the notion each time. Bernie never looked at the title to define her.

She was a leader, and she declared it every time she walked into a room. I watched how teachers, assistant principals, principals, and superintendents leaned into her ideas or moved out of the way like a matador when they saw her coming. She wielded natural power and influence. Bernie is open and honest. I need her in my life. She is my conscience, my critical friend, and my antithesis. Having a person or persons who can provide you with a different view of the world helps you learn and grow.

Kelly

In 1991, I was approached by the current president and several board members of the teacher's association in Fairfax, the Fairfax Education Association, to run for president. I had been active in the association for many years as a building representative and board member. I sat on and chaired several local and state committees. I lobbied the local county board, as well as state legislators. On May 2, 1991, I spoke to the Congressional Subcommittee on Education in Washington, DC. I was an advocate for the teaching profession, for my colleagues, and for what students deserved. When I was asked to consider running for office, I was excited about the contributions I could make but was afraid I might not have all the experience and skills in which to do it. I had less than ten years of teaching experience in the classroom and all the current board members had been around for quite a long time.

I recall being out of the loop many times when they were deep into nostalgia and talking about how things used to be. I honored that experience but also knew it was time for a new way of leading. The current president was part of that more experienced bunch and led by often being combative and aggressive. She was scrappy. That was not my style. I was also concerned about the future of my career. I had just finished my master's program and my internship as an assistant principal. I was on the road to becoming a school administrator.

I attended George Mason University as an undergrad and grad student. There was a beloved, yet unorthodox, professor by the name of Dr. D, as we affectionately called him. He taught several education leadership grad courses. I was lucky enough to have him for school law. His career in education included experience at all levels, elementary, middle, high school, and at the district level. He had a wealth of knowledge and experience. What I most admired about him was his generosity in sharing those experiences and providing "real world" applications to supplement the dry content contained in our textbooks. He was a master storyteller and used this talent to teach us not only the content required of the course but also to understand how that content translated to real-life leadership.

It was his willingness to be forthcoming and generous, use his quirky sense of humor, and take a genuine interest in our futures that led me to seek him out as a trusted advisor. When I wasn't sure what to do and with his vast and varied experience I knew he would be able to provide me with some wise counsel. I also considered the principal at my school to be a mentor and advisor in these times of tough decision-making.

I first approached my principal. I explained the decision I was struggling to make, run for President or continue to pursue a principalship. Without much discussion, she immediately shared her opinion. I should pursue a principal position. She had always been supportive in this endeavor and knew I was furthering my education for this purpose. She was surprised I was even considering any alternative. I believe wholeheartedly she had my best interest at heart when advising me the way she did. Something was missing in her advice. There was no real debate, and she asked very few questions. So although I had her valued opinion to consider, I was without an in-depth analysis of why that was the best decision for me at this time. I needed another opinion from someone who would challenge me on both opportunities.

I made an appointment to talk with Dr. D. I knew he had a breadth of experience and understanding to bring to this internal debate. I also knew he, too, had teacher advocacy and association experience. I went to his office, and he greeted me in his usual sarcastic way, "What do YOU want?"

I explained to him my dilemma—should I run for office or become a principal?

He smiled at me and said, "What a wonderful dilemma! Both are great options. Imagine having none?"

He proceeded to ask me questions. What interested me in running for office? Why did I want to be a principal? What impact did I want to make in both positions? How might I choose one and not close the door to the other? This is what I needed. Not his opinion, but rather coaching me to come to my own decision.

It was the question of how I might keep the door open to pursue both options that led me to my final decision. I decided to run for President of FEA. Dr. D. predicted that, depending on how I served in that position, a principalship would be open to me after my two years in office. If I chose the principalship, I would be on a new path and the door to holding elected office at the Association would most likely be forever closed.

What wise advice. Or, rather, what brilliant curiosity. I learned from Dr. D. that the answer to most of what I seek is inside me. Although, from time to time, I might need wise counsel from those who came before me, if I get curious enough, within myself I have all the answers I seek.

> *The inspiration you seek is already within you. Be silent and listen.*
>
> RUMI

Show Up as a Coconspirator!

Kendra

The time is now—time for us to create the necessary space for us to share our truths and begin to heal. For me, this is about rediscovering who I am and beginning a rebirth.

Kelly

And for me, this is about finding my voice and being courageous enough to take a stand.

We continue showing up for each other for our weekly talks, our plans to vacation and learn with each other, and our commitment to supporting women in educational leadership. But this means laying down your ego, choosing courage over what's easy and self-serving, and sacrificing what it takes to be in service to others, especially those most vulnerable and unlike you. We are continuing on the journey to do this. It is hard. It is hard when you see and feel the obstacles before you. It is hard when people doubt your worth, passion, and intentions. It is hard. But Glennon Doyle reminds us that we "can do hard things."

I visualize the current cycle of change and transformation we experience like that of being on a hamster or Ferris wheel going round and round, never arriving at a destination. Many national and state organizations are attempting valiantly to change the conditions and opportunities for women in school leadership. They are hosting conferences where we gather, tell our stories, network, and perhaps gain new insights and understanding we can take back with us. We seek and find other women to counsel us and serve as mentors and coaches.

These actions are all very necessary. But they aren't sufficient and are not increasing the number of women in senior positions fast enough. When we make a conscious decision not to show up fully and authentically in all our strengths and emotions or when we are trapped in cultures where it is neither a safe nor brave space for us to do so, we contribute to the perpetuation of our unhealthy socialization and stereotyping of women, especially women of color. When we don't experience the entire wheel of emotion from all of us, not just the nurturing, comforting, sensitive ones, but also those that are deemed as aggressive or angry, then when we do experience the breadth of our humanity, we are shocked.

We internalize the misogyny we experience. We call out another woman when she is expressing anger, frustration, and aggression. We create a stereotype because we have no other experience in which to understand. This especially happens to Black, Indigenous, and other Women of Color. It's both self-protective because it feels unfamiliar and an outcome of our socialization. The ultimate example is when a Black woman of Indian descent running for vice president and is debating with her White male opponent, and she must smile, mind her tone when being interrupted, and state kindly, "I am talking."

So, what next? Next, we stop waiting. We stop waiting to belong. We stop waiting to be invited to display the full array of human emotions, strengths, courage, and vulnerability required of all of us. We stop "leaning in" and instead disrupt systems so we can fully wrap ourselves around our humanity. Wrap ourselves in love and self-compassion. Wrap ourselves in our strengths. Wrap ourselves in the opportunities we seek. And wrap ourselves around one another to "stitch a new garment. One that fits all of humanity and nature."

The next section of the book is about how we show up courageously, navigate the "in-between," and begin building a thriving space for ourselves. Where are you in your journey of self-discovery, allyship, and coconspiratorship in the advancement of women in educational leadership?

Here are some questions to ponder as you become unwrapped:

1. Identify a courageous journey you will take for yourself and/ or for someone else. Why is this courageous?

2. Who is on your journey with you? You cannot do this alone.

3. What do you need to learn and how will you learn it?

4. Recall a conversation that changed the trajectory of your life.

5. What (and maybe who) are you willing to sacrifice on this journey?

6. Who or what are you fighting for?

Recommended actions to take.

1. Listen to the sisters in your circles. When they share instances of "isms," validate them and learn more about the experiences.

2. Do homework. As an educational leader, continue to learn. Read books, attend workshops and seminars, and listen to podcasts about showing up for women leaders.

3. Use the new learning for advocacy. Now it is time to do something from listening and learning. Take the tools that you have learned to speak up, out, and for your sisters. This may mean creating a safe space for leaders to talk about the challenges of being a woman leader or supporting her in the moment when there appears to be a real or perceived oppression.

A BRAVE NEW ENDING

When we deny the story, it defines us. When we own the story,
we can write a brave new ending.

— BRENÉ BROWN

GROWING UP, WE never really wanted for anything. We believed we had all we needed. A roof over our head, food on the table, an occasional gift on holidays or time away with extended family members or friends. Our basic needs were always met, and we were allowed a little extra from time to time. When I was young, I had no idea what the square footage of a house meant. I didn't know our cozy home was roughly over a thousand square feet. What was square footage? And I didn't know the size of our tiny cottage-like house required my parents to add a third small bedroom upstairs for my brother and an addition off the kitchen in order to make room for hosting family gatherings. My sister and I shared the main bedroom. Our dad installed a temporary partition down the middle of the room to create a sense of private space for each of us. All I knew, at the time, was we had all the space we needed. Space to gather and space to be alone. Originally the house had a small, screened porch that jetted out toward the driveway. After we moved in, my dad enclosed the porch to give us a tiny room to read, watch

TV as a family, or use as a guest room. Our home was not mighty in stature, but she was beautiful in decor. My mom has a keen eye for decorating, and our home was filled with beautiful things while at the same time comfortable.

My dad worked in the restaurant and hospitality industry, and my mom worked five days a week at a local steakhouse. After I graduated from high school, Mom took office jobs that provided better pay and benefits. It wasn't until I married and started my own family that I truly understood what was required to run a household. I realized my parents needed both incomes to meet our family's financial obligations. My brother is just twenty months older than me, and my sister is almost six years younger. My brother and I attended a Catholic coed high school not far from where we lived in Arlington, Virginia. My sister attended an all-girls Catholic High School on the other side of town.

In my high school, students came from all over the Northern Virginia region, and many were from highly influential and wealthy families. They were sons and daughters of doctors, lawyers, CEOs, business owners, and even politicians as we lived just outside of Washington, DC. They lived in areas of our community that had homes with long meandering driveways, pools and tennis courts in the backyard, and media rooms before media rooms were in vogue. We did not have any of those things, nor did we live in those neighborhoods. In contrast, both of my parents worked to be able to send us to those private Catholic schools.

During my freshman year on an early school dismissal day, I was invited to go to lunch and then shopping with a group of new girlfriends. I didn't have a "mall experience," and my mom and I did not "do the mall" together. We simply were not shoppers. When we did visit the mall, we shopped mostly out of necessity, with intention and purpose.

After lunch at the food court, the plan was to "do the mall." I had a few dollars in my pocket and my carefully prepared strategy was to look around, window shop, and possibly buy some small token for myself. It felt self-indulgent since whatever I would purchase was not going to be a necessity, but I didn't want to go home empty-handed under the watchful eyes of my new friends. I wanted to keep the peace inside myself and in front of them. I quickly realized my friends had another plan in mind. It was obvious that they had a very different mall experience. I remember being amazed at their ability to take stacks of clothes from the racks into the dressing room, try everything on, and purchase whatever they felt looked great on them. There was no pre-planned intention or purpose, and I was envious of how carefree and without much thought they made their purchases. The freedom in which they roamed from store to store trying on whatever their heart desired was breathtaking. This was an experience unfamiliar to me as shopping trips in my family were a strategic mission.

This is where I began my hustle to fit in. This was my first memory of feeling as though I didn't belong. One of these things was not like the others and it was me. I would never reveal my true story. I would choose to manage my shame by remaining silent and keeping my secret, ultimately keeping the peace with my friends. The truth was I could not afford to shop as unconsciously as they did. Rather, I created a story of not being able to make up my mind, state that I was saving for some other treasure, or that I would return with my mom later to try on the items I liked as I valued her opinion. They would never know the real story behind my hustle—that I could not afford it.

I would tell a similar story, or hustle, every time I was invited to the mall or even when, at times, I needed a ride home from school. In my family, we did not get a new car the day we received our driver's license. That was not true for most of the students in my high school. All you needed to do was take one look in the full-to-capacity student parking lot. This was the place where I would perfect my hustle to fit in or acclimate to the standard rather than belong. I grasped that if I wanted to be like my friends, do the mall, and offer gas money in exchange for a ride home, I would need to boost the amount of the few dollars inside my pocket and grow my current financial situation. I was also planning to attend college after I graduated high school. I knew I needed to start saving for my share of those expenses. I needed a job.

High school was not the genesis of my work experience. That history is long and varied. My first experience with paid employment began when I was in the eighth grade. I worked every Saturday as a receptionist at the rectory of the Catholic Church where my family attended Mass and I attended elementary school. When Cook, as we affectionately called her, went away for the weekend or on vacation, I would stand in and prepare meals for the priests in residence and their visitors. I learned from Father McMurtrie how to fry up crispy bacon and have it ready promptly after he officiated the 7:30 a.m. mass. After all, he had to make his morning tee time. Father was also the principal of the high school I would soon be attending. So, no pressure to get it right!

I kept that job until I started high school. I quit the summer between eighth and ninth grade, thinking I would need all my time to focus on my studies and extracurricular activities to build my college application resume. At least, that was the plan. After the shock of the girls' day out shopping experience, I realized I needed my own personal revenue stream. This meant scaling back on some of my clubs and activities in order to work after school a few days a week and on weekends.

Halfway through my freshman year, I got a job at the same steakhouse where my mother worked. That job contributed nicely to my financial well-being throughout high school. I worked a few nights a week after school and every Saturday. I saved enough for things I wanted but never enough to go on those long, spontaneous, unconscious shopping sprees.

After graduating high school, I attended George Mason University as a pre-law student. In my first semester, I took a class on human growth and development. The professor required an observational field experience where we would have an opportunity to witness the theories we were learning in class. I was assigned to a second-grade classroom in an elementary school located adjacent to the University. I chose this particular school based on its location near campus and my dorm. I did not yet have a car on campus. This elementary school was a short walk across the parking lot and through the woods.

My field experience assignment changed everything. And, little did I know at the time, it put in motion my lifelong commitment to public education. I was fascinated by how the teacher combined psychology, best teaching practice, and entertainment to engage her students in learning. She moved with precision in and out of assessing what students previously learned, presenting new material, and practicing expanding skill sets and understandings. She moved with the grace of a dancer around the room providing answers to specific questions, gently placing a hand on a shoulder to call a student's attention back to the task, and addressing the entire class about what she was observing.

I was smitten with those second graders and how they approached their lessons with enthusiasm, raw honesty, and humor. I was hooked and decided to change my major to elementary education. I wanted to do what she was doing. I committed myself to completing my BS degree and becoming a teacher. Once again, that all-too-familiar feeling of not having enough washed over me. What I witnessed in that classroom stirred in me an excitement for my future I had not felt before or with my chosen previous major, pre-law. My new desire to become an elementary teacher meant completing my degree which came with a financial cost. Once again, I needed a job.

I worked several jobs throughout my college career. I was a resident advisor in my dorm. As compensation, we received a free room and a discount on our meal plan. It did not, however, cover the total bill or all my other expenses. My parents agreed to pay only for the cost of classes. And I was grateful. The rest was on me to figure out. I had to purchase books, pay the remaining balance on my meal plan and those additional fees every University invents. Oh, and hopefully have the ability to subsidize a social life. I searched for jobs on campus since my transportation situation was not ideal. I took a job as the cashier at our campus cafeteria, and I was the first waitress at our on-campus pub, The Rathskeller. It was always a ruckus when the rugby team would come in for beers after practice or a match. They were loud and obnoxious. They were also hungry, thirsty, and had money. They tipped well.

Winter breaks were usually more than a month long. This was an ideal time to take a full-time seasonal job and earn what I needed to carry me through most of the next semester. One holiday break, I worked for an inventory company leading a team that counted everything from big-box items at a local wholesale members-only retail warehouse to nuts and bolts at a small business hardware store. And my summers were spent at Western Electric making rotary phones on an assembly line. It was redundant work. The same thing every day. My brother and I worked the evening shift from three to eleven every summer between college semesters.

Our short summer tenure at the telephone plant started the same way every season, with an unofficial initiation from the full-time employees. They would engage in a friendly discussion that was not meant to be a two-way conversation. The full-time workers described how our limited tenure at the plant would play out. We were not to make our quotas during our time on the line or their quotas would increase when we left. I spent five nights a week getting close to completing my required allotment of stringing wires through the handsets. When I was close to achieving my quota, I would read books under my workstation I brought from home for the rest of the night. I plowed through the latest books on best teaching practices preparing for the day I would student teach. I also used this time to sink into the latest summer beach-themed novels, romantic fantasies, or adventure stories that would take me and my imagination around the world.

My job was to string the wires through the handset, screw on the end caps, lay them carefully in a bin, and move them to the next station for further assembly. Sometimes, in-between reading, I would write little notes and insert them into the handset with the hope the person who purchased the phone would read it. A game I played to help pass the time.

In 1984, I graduated from George Mason University with my BS degree in early childhood education. Just as I was completing my student teaching, I started to search for a way to earn money before I was offered and accepted a full-time teaching job. My brother had been working at our local recreation center, Arlington County Recreation Department, as a day camp counselor, tennis instructor, and gym monitor. Once again, he was making what was considered "good money" at that time. The pay was approximately nine dollars an hour. More than most hourly wage jobs would pay.

I applied to be a day camp counselor the summer before my student teaching semester and again right after graduation. As my fellow graduates were planning trips to the beach, to go on cruises and adventures abroad, I would create another story about being needed at home and how I was looking forward to my "summer kids" at camp. I would create another hustle to avoid the shame of needing to work rather than go on vacation. I would be living back home with my parents, hoping to move out on my own as soon as I secured a full-time teaching position. I worked for two consecutive summers as a counselor for the six- and seven-year-old day campers. My education degree qualified me to be a group leader, supervising two other counselors.

We spent our days planning and implementing fun, entertaining, and educational activities for our young campers. We went on walking field trips to local parks for picnics and nature study, we tie-dyed way too many t-shirts, and we held a field day where the campers would compete in non-competitive competitions. Everyone got a trophy! One week per session we spent five nights at a sleep-away camp. There was no better preparation for taking control of an elementary classroom than supervising a group of six- and seven-year-olds on a five-day sleepaway camping trip, sleeping in platform tents, using outhouse latrines, and showering in outdoor facilities.

I graduated in the spring of 1984 with my bachelor's degree and was certified to teach pre-k and elementary students. After graduation, I applied to be a substitute teacher with Fairfax County Public Schools to get my foot in the door and start meeting principals who might have a vacancy for a young, eager elementary teacher. In January of 1985, I accepted a full-time second-grade substitute teaching job. The current teacher was pregnant with twins and would take immediate leave to go on bed rest. There was no co-teaching transition, and the class was immediately all mine. Approximately one month after I started my assignment the principal, Dr. Davidson, knocked on my door and asked me to come to see her after school. I racked my brain to figure out what I had done that required a visit to the principal's office.

After dismissal, I went reluctantly to see her, and she told me the full-time teacher was not returning and that Fairfax County Public Schools was pleased and excited to offer me the full-time position. The dream I had on that fortuitous day when I first walked into an elementary classroom to complete my assigned field experience had come true. I had the chance to create a place for students to come and engage in learning just like the teacher I observed. It was official. I was a teacher.

My history with work started very young and spans a variety of experiences. I can greet and welcome visitors to a church rectory office, cook, count widgets in big box and hardware stores, run a cash register in a cafeteria, serve uproarious rugby players, assemble telephone parts, and I can teach. I couldn't remember being without a job since the eighth grade. I was used to being very busy. Busy by this time was a measure of my worthiness. The busier I was and the more productive and money I earned, the more I felt worthy. Worthy of what? I wasn't really sure. My self-esteem was tied to this act of being a hard worker. A belief that would be a part of me for many years.

This was the "story" I had created all my life until I decided to leave my job at Gallup after almost sixteen years as an education consultant. It would turn out to be both a painful and unmistakable life-altering decision. It would blow my hustle wide open, exposing my shame and upending the very story I created that defined my worthiness. I didn't have another job waiting in the wings. That felt unfamiliar, paralyzing, outlandishly irresponsible, and frightening.

How would my decision impact our family's financial well-being? I contributed significantly to the family household income and was about to make a big dent in it.

There were so many questions whirling around my head. Was I being selfish, not caring about my family but solely about myself? Were things at work not as bad as they felt? Couldn't I just stay and keep the peace? What would I do next? I couldn't remember a time when I didn't have a professional purpose or reason to get up in the morning. I couldn't remember when I didn't have somewhere to go with people waiting and counting on me. Sure, I didn't love all my jobs, but the one I was doing with my school partners at Gallup I truly loved. It was the workplace culture that was causing me to suffer, and I didn't know at the time how to fix it. I believed I was the one who was broken and in need of fixing.

When I woke up that first morning with no job, I felt peculiar. My time was mine to do with as I pleased. I had no emails to respond to. I had no meetings and nowhere to go. For the first few days, I reveled in the long mornings. I lingered over my first cup of hot coffee as I slowly scrolled through the morning newspaper. That would be a hard copy newspaper where you actually turn page after page. I went for daily walks with and without our red dapple dachshund, Sadie. For the first couple of weeks, I felt like I was on a wonderful, relaxing vacation. One of those vacations I could never take in college because I was always working.

But like all vacations, that peaceful respite came to an end. I felt something was missing, gone as if there had been a death. I had no real reason to get out of bed, shower, or dress. I had nowhere to go, and no one was waiting to see me, talk with me, create with me. My husband, Steve, was on assignment out of the country and would be there for the next year. My oldest daughter, Madi, was working in Los Angeles. I was so proud of her for taking the risk to move across the country immediately after graduating from college. She was starting her career in social media. I had no idea what that meant at the time, but I did know LA was one of the cities where she needed to be to access opportunities. Shelby, my youngest, had returned to college early for her junior year. She was completing a leadership program and had to go back for a workshop before classes started. I was so proud of my family. They were being brave with their lives, making an impact, and doing what they loved and did best.

Days for me got longer. My morning coffee became more of a necessity from not sleeping the previous night than a wonderful anticipation. I discontinued my routine walks and blamed it on exhaustion. If it weren't for Sadie's irksome need to have to go out from time to time, I don't think I would have ventured outside at all. Friends and family invited me to meet them for meals out at our favorite restaurants and at their homes. On occasion, I accepted their invitation, and upon returning to a dark and lonely house, this deep, painful feeling of despair, and scarcity took my breath away like it does when jumping into a cold pool on a hot summer day. I broke down sobbing every time I returned home.

I spent most of my days in bed or laid out on the couch watching Anthony Bourdain take me to parts unknown. Bourdain was a celebrity chef and bestselling author of *Restaurant Confidential.* I learned from his exquisite writing to never order fish at a restaurant on Monday. The chef traveled to far-off unfamiliar locations and within the United States to teach about food, culture, and humanity. I would escape to the many exotic and not-so-exotic places where he would venture in his CNN show *Anthony Bourdain: Parts Unknown.* I made a mental list of all the remarkable places I wanted to visit in this world one day. The top of my list is Vietnam. His love for the culture, food, and people was palpable. I, too, acquired a love for the country through the television screen.

On June 8, 2018, Tony, as he was affectionately called, took his own life in the Le Chambard Hotel in France. The irony is painfully not lost on me. As Tony was suffering from his private demons, he was helping me evade mine. One evening, I was lying in bed watching an episode, and, as I rolled over to my left side, I felt a tug in my chest. During the day, I had attempted to return to my yoga practice and believed it to be a muscle that was angry with me for not showing up on my mat for such a long time. When I woke up the next morning, I didn't give it a second thought. I went about my day which involved TV adventures with Tony, frequent snacking rather than nourishing myself with delicious meals, and taking Sadie out when she begged long enough. This was my routine from sunup to sundown.

The next night, I felt the same tug in my chest. This time, it was more of a jolt or hard kick-like feel. I realized this was not a pulled muscle, but rather my heart beating hard and heavy but not rapidly. I was feeling individual heartbeats as if someone was inside my chest pounding to get out. I was scared. Really, really scared.

The next morning, after a night without sleep, I called a local cardiologist and asked for an appointment to see the doctor right away. When I described what I was feeling, the receptionist asked if I could come in that day. And I did. I saw Dr. Jeffery Luy. Dr. Luy was a very small, quiet, and gentle man. After an initial exam where I was responding to lots of questions, he decided more tests were needed. He started those tests by sending me home with a heart monitor and a clicker. For the next forty-eight hours, I was to click every time I felt that thud that lunged in my chest. I was clicking all day and especially at night. I returned with the monitor and completed a stress test, EKG, and ultrasound. Dr. Luy said he would have the results in a few days, and he wanted to see me the following week to review them together. And I was not to worry. Of course not. My heart is trying to escape and I am not to worry!

I returned to his office the following week to have my results read and reviewed. As I entered his office, Dr. Luy greeted me at the threshold of the exam room door with a warm smile. He invited me in, and rather than asking me to sit on the exam table, he asked me to take a seat on one of the chairs. He sat in the seat next to me, not behind his desk. At this point, I am thinking, *This is it! He has really bad news to tell me. I will need to ask Steve to return from overseas as he offered to do when I told him what I was experiencing. My girls will need to come home, and I will have to get my personal effects in order.*

Dr. Luy looked straight into my eyes. He has soft, kind eyes. I remember his words. He said, "Tell me what's going on. You are in great shape. All of your test results were exceptional and strong, and they all show normal heart functioning."

I thought, *How could this be? He is wrong. My heart is taking beats so hard I know you can see it through my t-shirt.*

He went on to explain in a way I could understand. "What you are experiencing is called PVC."

I only knew that as the white pipes used for plumbing.

"This stands for Premature Ventricular Contractions. Your heart is taking extra heartbeats that begin in one of your two lower pumping chambers. These extra beats disrupt your regular heart rhythm, sometimes causing you to feel a fluttering or a skipped beat in your chest. They are not life-threatening or debilitating. They are more annoying and startling from time to time. But you are not limited in doing anything you want to do."

So what did I want to do?

Dr. Luy went on to say, "They are often brought on by stress or anxiety. Do you have anything you want to share with me that might cause one or both of those?"

I looked again at those kind, empathetic eyes and began to cry. "Well, I quit the job I loved after nearly sixteen years. My husband is overseas on a dangerous assignment. My oldest daughter moved to LA. And my youngest is back at school. I don't know what to do with myself after not working since I was fourteen years old, and I am applying to a bunch of positions I have no interest in accepting if offered." By this time, my soft cry turned into an ugly cry.

Dr. Luy looked at me with warmth and understanding and said, "Oh, Kelly, just one of those things can cause PVC."

We spent some time talking. He didn't rush me out of his office, and, at the end of our conversation, we agreed the best course of action was for me to find a supportive therapist and consider medication that would help to calm me. Dr. Luy was the angel I needed, and I will be eternally grateful to him.

That night, Steve and I had our regularly scheduled FaceTime conversation. I had mentioned in one of our previous calls how I was feeling and that I had an appointment with the cardiologist. On this call, I explained the results of my tests and my PVC diagnosis and what caused it. He immediately said he was coming home. I loved him even more than I already did for that response. I reassured him I was going to be just fine and that I was searching for the right therapist. The following day, I told my daughters of my condition and the causes. I wanted them to know as young women that taking care of their mental health and well-being was as important as taking care of their physical health. I wanted to dismantle the stigma around seeking counseling and deciding to take medication in order to best care for ourselves as women. See, this too can happen to your mom. That was a gift I wanted to give them.

I shared my diagnosis with a trusted friend, and she encouraged me to follow the plan. Find a therapist that worked for me. One with whom I could offload my emotions, my anxiety, grief, and fear. One who would recommend the right combination of medication. My friend also recommended a book for me to read. She knew I was an avid reader and loved to escape in books, fiction, and nonfiction. She talked to me about Brené Brown's work on shame, vulnerability, and courage. She suggested I read her best seller, *Rising Strong*. I purchased it that day. This was my second miracle intervention. I replaced my daily dates with Anthony Bourdain and "Parts Unknown" with ones with Brené and devoured every word she wrote. She talks about how, if we are brave, daring, and want to be courageous with our lives we will also experience failure, heartbreaks, and disappointment. That should not prevent us from doing those things we are called to do in the way we are called to do them.

I was reminded of a quote by Audre Lorde, "When I dare to be powerful—to use my strength in the service of my vision—then it becomes less and less important whether I am afraid," As I read Brené's book, I wrote notes in the margins, dog-eared pages, and highlighted the parts I would put to use right away. I purchased a journal and began to write about my last twenty-four months at Gallup, what I knew to be true and what I was making up in my head. I discovered where I needed more data and understanding before I could conclude what actually happened. And then I read the line that changed everything for me, as it did for Brené: *It's not the critic who counts*. This magical, crazy thinking comes from the Theodore Roosevelt speech known as "The Man in the Arena."

Brené discovered it when she was going through her own self-described "spiritual awakening." And it was precisely what I needed to hear. I was spending so much time in deep depression trying to figure out why I wasn't enough. I did everything that was asked of me and more. I was the top mid-level market consultant. I redefined what our division could be by bringing in high revenue and producing impactful projects, resulting in greater visibility and opportunity for the company. I spent decades of my life creating the perfect hustle I thought would be impenetrable and allow me to fit in. It was supposed to keep the peace.

And yet, I was never fully accepted by the in-crowd or by "legacy" company leaders. The defense I created by hiding behind hard work and busyness was no longer working for or serving me. As if it ever did. Why did I find myself in dire need to leave the very job I loved, the clients I truly cared about, and one at which I was damn good at? I felt guilty for engaging in similar behavior as my "critics" and felt that I somehow deserved what I got. This thinking only served to hurl me into a depression I didn't realize I was in. I thought it was normal and okay to lay in bed all day watching a CNN docuseries and various rom-coms, and then at night cry a cleansing cry that rocked me finally to sleep.

I wonder to this day how one researcher from the University of Houston could look so deeply into my soul, know, and understand exactly what I was feeling and not feeling, and understand the very skills, words, learning, and practices I needed to get me back on my feet again and launch me into an entirely new way of moving through the world. With therapy, the right medication, and a process to offload and work through my experience and pain, I slowly dismantled my hustle and began to discover who I was authentically. I put down the heaviness of trying to keep the peace. I was beginning to unwrap my conditioning and experiences. I was on my way to writing a second life chapter.

Most education leadership programs are still very traditional. When I was in my master's degree program earning my principal certification, my courses were primarily focused on four things: compliance, policy and regulation, data, and law. Nowhere in any of my classes did I learn how to be a courageous school leader. Nowhere did I acquire the language I could use when engaging in hard conversations. Nowhere did I learn how a woman leader could speak up for herself, ask for what she wanted and needed, and understand how to show up with all her unique strengths and talents. In fact, I would venture to guess most of us have never been taught these skill sets. For the majority of us, it would be safe to assume our conditioning was designed to keep the peace.

We create our own kind of hustle to fit in, fix ourselves when we don't need fixing, and acclimate rather than show up authentically demanding to belong. This is true of women as a collective and is especially true of Black, Indigenous and other Women of Color who have been historically sidelined in the workplace. System leaders create rules, spoken and unspoken, dictating how women, and especially women of color, are mandated to show up. How to wear our hair, how to dress, how to speak, how to behave in team meetings, and how to react when we disagree. And for systematically marginalized women, workspaces are not safe, and the only option to thrive is to fit in or assimilate to cultural norms.

Women have made efforts to unwrap ourselves from these tethers. We spend time gathering at conferences targeted at women education leaders. We mentor and counsel one another. These efforts are necessary but not sufficient. The number of women in senior-level school positions and our longevity in those positions has not significantly improved since the late 1990s. What are we missing? In her best-selling book *Untamed*, Glennon Doyle tells us,

> *There is no one way to live, love, raise children, arrange a family, run a school, a community, a nation. The norms were*

created by somebody, and each of us is somebody. We can make our own normal. We can throw out all the rules and write our own. We can build our lives from the inside out. We can stop asking what the world wants from us and instead ask ourselves what we want for our world. We can stop looking at what's in front of us long enough to discover what's inside us. We can remember and unleash the life-changing, relationship-chang-ing, world-changing power of our imagination. It might take us a lifetime. Luckily, a lifetime is exactly how long we have.

How do we embark on the path of breaking down the norms in schools, districts, and on-campus that were created by someone else? How do we begin to dismantle how schools were founded and create a place for all humanity to thrive? What do we need to "unleash the life-changing, relationship-changing, world-changing power of our imagination" inside each one of us? As I was reading Brené's words, I was discovering new skill sets, words, and ways of showing up and asking for what I want and need. These were like the gifts I used to buy for my mom all wrapped up in a big ass bow.

Do you ever wish you could have a moment in life to do over? I do. I didn't know how to show up and respond to what was hap-pening at Gallup. I needed the skills, words, and understanding of what it means to be brave and fearful and to still initiate hard conversations. I needed to know how to be vulnerable, to align my behaviors with my values, to require others to be responsible for their behaviors, to learn how to trust and how to be cautious with my trusting, and most importantly, put it all together and learn how to keep on going even when I come up short. I believe I would have handled my job situation very differently had I only known how to do so.

If I knew then what I know now, if I had the words I have now, and if I had the skills, I believe to have been vital to ending my hustle and conditioning, the ending would have been different for me at Gallup. That is not to say I would have stayed. But the conversations would most definitely have been different and the struggle following my departure would perhaps not have been as great.

In her best-selling book, *The Fix, Overcome the Invisible Barriers That Are Holding Women Back At Work*, Michelle P. King, talks about the success "prototype" at work. Most workplaces, including schools, were not built by women or for women and the conditions required to thrive in leadership positions were not created with us in mind. Most were built around a "prototype," as King describes it, of what is required to be a successful worker and leader. The model of the ideal school or district leader is male, White, cisgendered, able-bodied, and married with support from a wife at home. Leaders who do not fit this ideal must be "fixed." Our challenge, therefore, is to figure out how to fit into the acceptable norm for whom the workplace was created and how to demonstrate leadership that might look different and similarly, if not more, impactful.

School governing bodies and school boards expect a woman to perform her role in exactly the same way as the man who came before her, never taking into consideration differences in obligations, social standards, and overall well-being. We simply plow ahead, work hard, mimic the "prototype," and hope we don't fall apart in the pursuit of high standards and achievement. We are told if we just work hard enough, we can achieve what we dream and desire. The idea of meritocracy, if you work hard you will succeed, is just bullshit. The women I know in education leadership are some of the hardest working people I have ever met. Yet the data behind selection, promotion, and retention of women in senior leadership positions tell a different story. So what part of our story isn't being told?

As women leaders in education, we do battle patriarchy. All too often we are menaced with acts of misogyny that we either ignore, laugh off, or internalize and pass on to other women. We care deeply and forego our own desires and needs all in the name of selflessness. Case in point, take a look at the data on the effects of the pandemic on women. Women's job loss rate is 1.8 times that of the mean job loss due to the pandemic. In the United States specifically, unemployment data show that 11.2 percent of women lost their jobs, compared to 7.9 percent of men.

In December 2020, 140,000 jobs were lost. All belonged to women. The data clearly shows women assumed the greater load and share of household responsibilities including the education of their children during the pandemic while experiencing a greater loss in income and economic power. As we begin—as a nation, districts, and schools—to re-emerge from this long health nightmare, we must examine the impact on women being the social safety net for our communities and for our country. We are forced back into our socially expected roles and, in doing so, we suffer.

Kate Manne, philosopher and author of *Down Girl, The Logic of Misogyny*, tells us "the human givers are expected to offer their time, attention, affection, and bodies willingly, placidly, to the other class of people, the human beings." We give and give and give in order for others to be more fully human. All the while we are sacrificing our own full humanity. So we do the most. We do the most at home for those we care about and love. And we do the most at our work without causing discomfort for others and remaining silent about our own needs. And it benefits the system. When we ask for our fair share, we are directed and instructed on how to "fix" ourselves. I submit that women school leaders don't need fixing. The system does. And women need new skill sets and words, and a reconditioning of how we were raised and believe we should show up in this world. Together, as allies, accomplices, and coconspirators we can disrupt the system and write a magnificent and courageous new ending to our collective story.

We must continue to gather but in a brand new way. We have been mentoring one another. We are creating networks where we recommend each other for positions, and we assemble to offload our frustration, grief, and anger. Mentorship and networking are important, but it is simply not enough. It's time to stop denying the stories of our collective experience.

I love the idea of "constructive discomfort" as described by Scott Senenshein in his book, *Stretch*. I think about the women who are constructively disrupting systems, telling their stories, writing new brave endings, and in doing so making the future better for other women to enter the arena. I think of Senator Tammy Duckworth. Senator Duckworth is an Iraq War Veteran and Purple Heart recipient. She served on active duty in 2004 in Iraq. Her helicopter was shot down by a rocket-propelled grenade, and she ultimately lost both her legs and almost lost her right arm.

Tammy Duckworth is the Senator from Illinois who can be seen in her wheelchair around the Capital and DC as she works to better the lives of the citizens she represents and all Americans. She is the first Thai American woman elected to Congress. Her military record is admirable. But it's not her only noteworthy accomplishment. In 2018, she gave birth to her youngest daughter and became the first senator to do so while in office. Now that posed an interesting dilemma in the Senate. Senate rules prohibited children from coming onto the Senate Floor. Shortly after Senator Duckworth found out she was pregnant, she began to coconspire with her friend and colleague, Senator Amy Klobuchar. Senator Klobuchar is a White women born in Plymouth, Minnesota, and represents that state. She talked about what she needed and Senator Klobuchar listened. Then she went into action and assisted Senator Duckworth in manipulating a rule change. This strategy would require Senators to vote in person.

Senator Klobuchar, at the time, was on the Senate Rules Committee and was the perfect accomplice for this act of "constructive disruption." On the day before the Senator's new baby daughter would make her first appearance on the Senate floor, a vote was set. Senators, both Republican and Democrat, voted unanimously that, in the future, all senators would be permitted to bring infants up to age one into the chamber. This was no small achievement. No matter the objection or obstacle, the two women persisted and eventually changed the rule for all future women who serve in the United States Senate. Senator Duckworth was quoted in one article as saying, "It's about time." Together, as coconspirators and accomplices in disrupting the system, Senator Duckworth and Senator Klobuchar wrote a new brave ending. They began the unwrapping.

We can do the same, and now it's our turn to disrupt the system of education and the cultures that reside inside school districts and on campuses. It is time to become unwrapped. It's time we find our voice with new words, ask for what we need, stay in hard conversations, show up authentically as we define what that means, and create a whole new way of leading. And we must show up as a collective for one another and as allies first and then accomplices and coconspirators. I believe schools, teachers and staff, students, and our communities will be better off for having done so.

Questions to ponder as you become unwrapped:

1. **Audre Lorde** tells us, "When we speak, we are afraid our words will not be heard nor welcomed, but when we are silent we are still afraid, so it is better to speak." Go back to your origin story. In what moments did you experience failure, a bad decision, heartbreak? We can experience our greatest amount of growth in those moments. What did you learn? How will you use that experience and what you learned to be braver in work and life?

2. How do you want to be braver in your life and work? As with anything we do, including learning new leadership skills, it's easier if we tackle it in small doses. So consider how you might want to be 5 percent, 10 percent, or 20 percent braver.

3. What can you do tomorrow to be a more daring and less protective leader? How will you know you did what you said you would do? Create accountability for yourself.

4. How can you move from being an ally to an accomplice? From an accomplice to a coconspirator? For those who have privilege, how can you leverage it to benefit other women?

5. Identify three-to-five women you have built trust with and can rely on to provide meaningful feedback. Create your own internal team of coconspirators and constructive disruptors. These will be your integrity partners. You don't have to go it alone.

THE IN-BETWEEN

Black women can feel more whole not just by carving out spaces
where they can speak and act in the ways that feel most natural,
but also by embracing every facet of their unique beauty.

— JONES AND SHORTER-GOODEN

IMAGINE WAKING UP every day and laying out three outfits. There is the "one." This is the outfit that you love to wear. It feels comfortable. You wear it with ease, having it slide over your head and shoulders like silk. You do not have a care in the world what people think about it. It is cozy, warm, and makes you feel like you. You snuggle yourself into it and feel the most relaxed. Then you have the other outfit, the "suit." It is a bit restrictive. It feels awkward when you first put it on but then as the day goes by, you get used to it. Occasionally, you have to readjust, straighten it, and dust it off, but it does not feel too foreign to wear. Sometimes, you prefer to wear it over your comfy outfit. It gives you a feeling of importance and belonging.

Then, there is the third outfit. This is the one that is the most restrictive. It feels like heavy armor. You wear this one when you go into battle. It shields you from the blows, and at times, you can retreat into it and become invisible. Here is the thing. You long to wear your cozy outfit, but you only wear it for people who have earned the right to see you in it—family, spouse, significant other, children, best friends, mentors, mentees, and so on.

Now, imagine that you change these outfits several times a day depending on the situation and environment. Sometimes, the outfits can change within minutes of each other. Pure exhaustion! Yet, I don't know how to turn this off and only wear my comfy clothes. As a Black woman, I am constantly navigating and changing these "outfits." And while people typically navigate their environments based on several social and situational cues, I navigate these spaces with a race and gender lens.

In 1989, Dr. Kimberle Crenshaw coined the term *intersectionality*, which refers to the theory of how overlapping or intersecting social identities, particularly minority identities, relate to systems and structures of oppression, domination, or discrimination.[33] These layers of identity, especially for women and people of color, cannot be isolated. The coalescing of these identities is the idea that you cannot treat Black women as purely women or purely Black. This would ignore the unique challenges that Black women face as a group. As a researcher and law professor, Dr. Crenshaw has spent over thirty years lecturing about critical race theory and intersectionality and has responded to conservative critics who believe that she is purporting a new hierarchy where Black women would be on top. Imagine that! Well, the institution and structure are not set up to perpetuate a new dominant structure, and the fact that people fear an overthrow of this structure is precisely what is wrong with it. It is meant to divide and oppress. So, these overt and covert structures and ideas are what I have to contend with daily. How can I be my authentic self, knowing

---

33   Kimberle Crenshaw, "Demarginalizing the Intersection of Race and Sex: A Black Feminist Critique of Antidiscrimination Doctrine, Feminist Theory and Antiracist Politics" (University of Chicago Legal Forum, 1989).

that authenticity will be scrutinized from all angles including race and gender? I live in a space called the "in-between."

I come from a long line of women who spoke their minds and were the primary decision-makers in the family. These matriarchs were honored, and their words of wisdom were gold. My upbringing and experiences were the training ground for how I lead and engage in relationships today. I have also exerted a lot of energy defending who I am and who I aim to be. How I show up depends on people's perceptions of me, especially as a Black woman.

"You are bossy."

"You are loud."

"Why are you so angry?"

When I hear these statements/questions, I am not surprised. They are laden with gender and ethnic stereotypes that I have learned to navigate. These are part of my life lessons as a Black woman. As a young girl, I had "the talk"—not the talk that most typical White teenagers have with their parents. Our talk was about how to engage the police if pulled over (while walking, driving, hanging out with friends), how to respect "authority" so as not to be a victim of racial profiling, lessons taught for generations and emphasized during Jim Crow. This is how you increased the likelihood that you would leave the interaction physically unscathed. I learned how to talk slowly and drop my voice when addressing the police. You say, "Yes, sir" or "No, sir," keeping your hands where they can see them at all times. Stay calm! And, in an interesting juxtaposition, my mother taught me to speak up, advocate for myself, know my rich history, and fight for my rights. How do I balance these two lessons? I learned to navigate the intersectionality or the "in-between"—being cognizant of my surroundings and understanding the unwritten rules.

I use "in-between" because that is what it feels like. The moment when I have to decide which outfit I need to put on. Wearing the outfit is the easy part but deciding which one to put on requires so much emotional, psychological, and physical energy that the weight can be overwhelming. It is a mixture of trepidation, courage, resilience, risk, and exhaustion. And yet, I do it. I don't know any other way to be. I want to engage in what Sonya Renee Taylor purports as radical self-love. A love of self frees you from the confines of what others think, what you have been led to believe about yourself, and truly embraces that you are valued simply because you exist.

This is one of the reasons why I became an educator, especially in the neighborhood where I grew up. I wanted to educate students about navigating the "in-between"—teaching them to lean on their talents and strengths and recognize the perceived negative narratives of Black, Indigenous, and People of Color (BIPOC). I wanted them to learn the unwritten rules by which they played so that they could become aware of how to navigate them, giving them power and control over the choices that they will make.

As I am learning and growing in my own leadership and being, I am recognizing that this may not be the best move. It is safe. It is practical. But I was merely teaching people to survive and not thrive. Dr. Bettina Love states, "the life of survival is not living." In her book, *We Want to Do More Than Survive: Abolitionist Teaching and the Pursuit of Educational Freedom*, Dr. Love insists that to move from surviving to thriving an essential element of an abolitionist teacher is *mattering*.[34] Mattering is the feeling that we're a significant part of the world around us, it's the belief that we're *noticed*, *important*, and *needed*—right now.[35] This is complicated when the American structure refuses to value the Black body. This is made

---

34   Bettina Love, *We Want to Do More than Survive: Abolitionist Teaching and the Pursuit of Educational Freedom* (Beacon, 2020).
35   G. Elliott, Suzanne Kao, and A. Grant, "Mattering: Empirical Validation of a Social-Psychological Concept: Semantic Scholar," *Self & Identity*, 2004.

even more complex when identities cannot be isolated from one another; so Black and female create a challenging mix for me to navigate a world hell-bent on breaking me, unintentionally and intentionally.

During my tenure as a teacher, principal, coach, and now facilitator of leadership learning, I became interested in learning more about social psychology and the implications on leader development. I participated in several professional learning opportunities and earned certifications in four areas related to strengths, talent management, fierce conversations, and behavioral styles. While each learning experience affirmed my talents, personality traits, learning, and behavioral style, I also learned that these identifiers were not neutral. My talents and strengths had a different connotation when I showed up as a Black woman, and I knew that if I did not call out the cultural context by which we show up with these identifiers, I was leading and developing people blindly, especially my BIPOC sisters. I knew, from observation and personal experience, that it could be dangerous to ask a Black woman to simply "lean in" to a conversation without an awareness of the "in-between." Yet, my own experiences have left deep scars that tell the story of how these lessons were learned—mostly through trial and error. How I show up is never neutral or impartial. My Blackness does not render me invisible, yet the forces around me try to erase my presence, my value, my being.

I recall being "scolded" for sharing my thoughts at a meeting because that is "not how we do it here in the South, dear . . . [women] listen and know that the questions asked are rhetorical." This was a new lesson to learn—added to the laundry list of nuanced behaviors I have adapted. So, not only did I have to navigate my Blackness and my femaleness, but I also had to now navigate southernness, as well. The space "in-between" is narrow, and, at times I feel like I am being squeezed, but I am reminded of the strengths and power that come with knowing how to balance this space. Charisse Jones and Dr. Shorter-Gooden state in their book *Shifting*, "Though Black women in America frequently find confidence, and the voice, to inveigh against racism, too often these same women feel they must stifle themselves—and bury their pain-when being female, rather than being Black, is at the core of their mistreatment."[36] Sharing these realities became part of my mission, part of the awakening to the realities of how cultural biases paralyze and/or empower us.

I remember when I made the purposeful shift to lead and facilitate learning by exposing these realities for Black women like me—by being vulnerable. It began when Kelly shared an article with me called "Strengths So White: Interrogating StrengthsQuest Education Through a Critical Whiteness Lens" by Tapia-Fuselier and Irwin. Kelly and I had been talking about ways to focus our leadership development on the person within their context. One day, she emailed me the article and said, "Look at this! Tell me what you think."

The article shed light on what I have been silently wrestling with supporting educational leaders of color.

"I was told I need to tone down my emotions,"

"Am I coming across as too pushy?"

"I was told I had to cut my locs before I can be a leader in this district," or, "They say I am not polished."

After reading the article, I was approached by a colleague who was thinking about redesigning his professional development program. He was disturbed by the acts of violence he was seeing against Black men and women, and he wanted to talk. Now, at first, I was not open or even in the right state of mind to begin teaching

36   Charisse Jones and Kumea Shorter-Gooden, *Shifting: The Double Lives of Black Women in America* (Perennial, 2004). p. 38

White folx why I matter. My emotions were raw, and I was tired. After listening to him talk about his commitment to revise his work to address inequities within social sciences, I became curious. We talked for about two hours. I shared the idea of the "in-between," and he asked if I could write a blog to share this experience. In addition, he wanted to extend the conversation to a broader audience and engage in virtual conversation about how I wrestle with the perceived labels of being an "Achiever" or "Controller" as a Black woman. How these labels might work for a man or White folx, but not for women and marginalized communities. These adjectives contain negative connotations that perpetuate a stereotype.

I had never shared these specific thoughts explicitly to a larger audience, and I had not written about them. This was both a challenge and therapeutic. He scheduled a live Zoom session one Tuesday afternoon and I was the featured speaker. I remember getting dressed for the live broadcast interview. I was nervous, the nervousness that you get when everything is sweating. I pride myself on my ability to speak in front of people and even impromptu. But this was different. This was deeply personal and risky; I would be sharing my inner thoughts and feelings with an audience of strangers while being interviewed by a White man. In essence, I was sharing my experience of how men like him see me, treat me, and think about me. I was not sure how he would respond. Would he be defensive, make excuses, provide a rationale, or simply listen? As I spoke, my mouth felt like I was chewing cotton balls. The room was foggy. *Get it together!*

I inhaled deeply and said, "I want to recognize my ancestors and all of the women before me. I stand on their shoulders and ask them for the strengths to share my story." As I continued to speak, I began to shed the fear. After the interview, I thanked my friend for making the space and I thanked the virtual audience for listening.

Within one minute, my email was dinging and there was a knock at the door. My colleagues, friends, family, and strangers shared how connected they felt to the story. That the description of the "in-between" resonated with them. As I shared more of my story and embedded it in the professional learning and coaching, it was freeing for me to see the faces of women light up, their shoulders relax, and the silent acknowledgment that they are being seen.

Now, this does not mean there is no risk involved in this move. I usually get a few raised and furrowed eyebrows from men and White folx who feel on edge. Welcome to my world! I like the challenge of uncomfortable learning spaces because it means that learning can happen. Now, I am not talking about imposing guilt or shame. I am talking about sharing my personal, professional story that leads to what Susan Scott called *Fierce Conversations*—conversations that enrich a relationship. Not everyone will take the bait and engage in these conversations because I just shifted the power by empowering myself and the others in the room. I hope that a bit of my truth crept into their minds and left them wondering or maybe even listening to a little more than before. For my sisters in the room, their eyes told the story—the story of pain, frustration, exhaustion, and fed-upness. I do not purport that I have any answers, just an acknowledgment that I saw them and understood their pain, their secret battle, and a promise of sisterhood that could help us to find our rightful place at the table.

So, you may be asking, "Is that it? How do I get that seat and be at the head of the table?"

There is no set of strategies or tools that I can share that are universal for navigating the "in-between." Each person has a different set of circumstances. Some are very complicated and covert, and others are hardly impactful. The first thing I recommend that you do is to engage in recovery, rediscovery, and self-love.

Recovery

This interruption of who you think you are and the partial lapse in authenticity leads to a life of mask and suit-wearing and appeasement. There is a point in your life journey where the mask no longer fits. It is worn, weighty, and uncomfortable. You know that you are off-kilter but too afraid to be authentic. This is when you know it is time to declare—I have a problem! Step one in the recovery process is declaring who you are and admitting that you have a problem. I took an initial step in 1996 when I shaved my hair. It is one way to start over by stripping the process weight from my body. Now, this was simply one step in a series of steps. At the time, it was a physical step I took to get back to my roots. It was freeing and led to a series of steps along the way to feel and be free to be me. I remember running my fingers over my head and feeling the warmth and coolness on my scalp. I left the salon, took the bus, and rode through the streets of New York City with my head pressed against the window. I smiled as the sun warmed my face. People on the bus looked at me with smiles. It was as if they knew that I was in recovery and their smiles were the assurance that I was on the right journey.

I recall when I went to school that the comments I received from my students were mixed. Some really liked the natural look and others thought my relaxed, processed hair made me more beautiful. I am not judging people who choose to process their hair, but my students thought that the previous version of me was "more beautiful." Since then, I have relapsed with other forms of unwrapping that I have battled. These are real and perceived. The one thing I know for sure is how the road of recovery can look and feel. This helped me bounce back when I became ready again. This toggle between my comfortable state and "pretend me" state varied based on the environment and situation.

Rediscovery

I was lost along the way. During my years in college and early in my professional career, I did everything I could to fit in, especially when I became a leader. I wanted there to be no doubt that I warranted the job, role, and respect. I made sure that I dressed the part, talked the part, and met everyone's expectations. Jones and Shorter-Gooden call this the "myth of inferiority." They state that though we are educated, and may have come from homes more prosperous than our counterparts, "outsiders still often react with surprise then Black women are well-spoken, inquisitive, or well-read...the phrase, 'You're so articulate,' while seemingly a compliment, the underlying message is that is it surprising to find an intelligent Black woman who speaks Standard English so well."[37] I have heard these statements and they have been told to me.

There is a difference in how this has been spoken to me, though. I recall one moment when a colleague was describing a woman he had met at a conference. He said, "Oh, she was tall in stature, well-dressed, and very articulate." Now, on the surface, you may not see or understand how this cuts, but when describing other attendees, there were no descriptors, simply their names. In the world of leadership, there are even more pronounced disparities in describing Black women in leadership versus their White counterparts. This always takes me back to the scene in Spike Lee's *Do the Right Thing* when Mookie asks Pino why most of his favorite artists, sports figures, and musicians are Black. Pino responds, "They are Black but not really Black. They are more than Black. It's different. To me, it's different." Somehow this story of "acceptable Black" creeps in to be the defining exception to the social rule about who we are

---

37   Charisse Jones and Kumea Shorter-Gooden, *Shifting: The Double Lives of Black Women in America* (Perennial, 2004). p. 17.

which also elevates the desire to fit in. This constant yearning for approval and belonging fed my desire to fit in.

Now, there comes a time when you realize that no matter how hard you try to appease others, there still is an emptiness. You can feel it in the pit of your stomach. Remember, this is a process. While in the throngs of my career, I was navigating a lot of internal and external forces with many political implications. As the environment shifts and I become more entrenched in the organization, the navigating of the "the in-between" becomes even more pronounced. This is when a series of additional steps are taken to discover who you are. This goes much deeper than shaving my head. This requires mentorship and aligning myself with an affinity group. This is where I get educated. Over the past twenty-five years, I have been connecting with peers, classmates, mentors, and my elders, learning about their life journeys and gaining insight from their personal stories of struggle and perseverance.

The year 2020 was pivotal for my rediscovery. COVID-19, the televised killing of George Floyd and Amaud Aubery, the senseless murder of Breonna Taylor, and the most divisive presidential election I have ever experienced led to deep reflection about my life as a Black woman, wife, and mother. The quiet at home and the deafening societal noise had me going from zero to ten in a matter of six months. I questioned my value, my worth; not within the eyes of others, but within my eyes. What stand was I going to make? I began reading three books a month and listening to a series of podcasts, searching for ways to help me understand what I was experiencing. I am not a consistent journal writer, but I began noting my feelings in my big red book—my beloved book of ideas, poems, and statements. I began to write simple statements to help grapple with my feelings during the week. These statements were life lessons taught to me through cultural nuances and by the women who had the most influence on who I was becoming.

Statements like:

"It be that way sometimes,"

"It is what it is,"

"I just can't,"

"Oh, no you didn't," and

"Keep yo' hands on the steering wheel."

These statements and countless others tell the story of the lives of Blacks and Black women wrestling with the day-day struggles of existing. One weekend, I decided to take the statements and turn them into t-shirts. T-Shirt Statement Saturday was born. Each Saturday, I wear a t-shirt that represents my feelings at the moment. I take a picture and add a caption. In addition, I record brief explanations of the statements to memorialize the lessons taught. It is an opportunity for me to wrestle with what's on my mind and expose myself - practice vulnerability. I continue *#tshirtstatement* today and the "movement" is growing. Women and men respond with their t-shirt statements, telling their personal stories or supporting me through my rediscovery. It is very spontaneous and off the cuff, so my thoughts are raw and in the moment. It has been exhilarating and affirming because I realize I am not alone in my thoughts. Many women are rumbling with the same struggles, trying to navigate in a world of "in-betweens."

My story is the story of many others who are also grappling with how to explain how they are feeling. These statements have become my declaration as well as my step in taking back my life. It's my voice speaking over the din and permeating the walls of oppression. I now have allies and what Betina Love calls coconspirators to help me in my recovery. There is power in numbers. Next stop, self-love.

Self-Love

This is where I want to reach. I am not there yet, but I am making progress. This is the hardest step. We are bombarded with millions of images of beauty, acceptable behavior, and our place as women in society. And the battle to determine my own beauty standards is entrenched in my learned beliefs and values. So, I am exploring what that is. There has been a spiritual awakening and I am feeling a pull toward my African roots. I am not sure what it is and what it means. But to understand this pull is to understand the historical context of the Black female image in American culture.

Throughout slavery in America, Black women have been objectified as lazy, domestic, oversexed, hysterical beasts who need to be tamed. I use these terms to illustrate the paradox in the descriptions because Black women were the backbone of American slavery. They were primary breeders, mistresses, and workers both in the field and in the master's home. Their Black bodies were abused and yet they still "kept" their own families (at least the ones they were allowed to keep or create). In contrast, White women were deemed pure and the ideal model of beauty, purity, and modesty. As the number of children born to slave masters increased, the threats and treatment of Black women continued to morph into conniving, oversexed gypsies who used witchcraft to take over the minds of slave masters rendering them "not accountable" for their behaviors. White women amplified the notion that Black female slaves poisoned their husbands compounding the consistent physical and sexual abuse of Black women. As the images of Black women morphed, the stain of the image of the mischievous promiscuous woman or the "Mammy" caricature figure persisted.

For young Black girls, the hypersexualization of their bodies and the expectation that they are destined to struggle and fail is juxtaposed with the notion that they are expected to "grow up" faster and take care of the household, sacrificing their girlhood. Mikki Kendall, in her book *Hood Feminism*, describes the idea of *adultification*, the "racist practice of children of color as significantly older than they are...removing the possibility of innocence from young girls, especially Black girls."[38]

Kendall goes on to explain that to dispel these stereotypes, Black girls and women participate in the culture of "respectability" politics and narratives to justify their place and rights within the dominant culture. The problem with this approach is that it places all of the work on the marginalized community to solve the equity issue, placing the blame and responsibility on Black women for not "fitting in." Imagine this weight. This generational weight is compounded and disguised to perpetuate the initial idea of the Black woman. This is what I navigate daily, the negative images in videos and print; the lack of Black women decision-makers who do the grunt work to make the boss look good; the fixers of societal ills, the caregivers and nurturers; and the fierce and strong woman who can grin and bear it. The mental, emotional, and physical exhaustion of bouncing between competing priorities and expectations led to a perpetual state of internal and external flux. The "in-between" is real and navigating this space takes skills that have been part of my life because, as my great grandmother would say, "It be that way sometimes."

So, envision the space between a rock and a hard place. The "in-between" is that space. It is where I learned the necessary survival skills, and, for forty-nine years, I have been surviving, learning the moves to be made to stay safe, fit in, and minimize trouble. Jones and Shorter-Gooden say that "Black women are yoga masters.

---

38   Mikki Kendall. *Hood Feminism: Notes from the Women That a Movement Forgot.* (New York: Penguin Books, 2021). p. 76.

We're required to bend in as many different ways as possible in our daily activities. We have to be extremely flexible and people expect us to be good at it—friends, family, relatives, coworkers, society."[39] Here is where I lost myself as well. Assimilating to a world I was hoping would accept me into its illustrious club. So, how do you engage in self-love? Sonya Renee Taylor, author of *The Body Is Not an Apology: The Power of Radical Self-Love,* states that it begins with your heart "calling you toward something exponentially more magnanimous and succulent than self-esteem or self-confidence." [40]

You see, I don't see these false images of Black women in my head or feel the perpetrated negativity in my heart. I see bright hues of purple, royal blue, and sea green fabric blowing in the wind like ribbons. The glow of milk chocolate skin and the regal features of the women standing shoulder to shoulder float in my head as a reminder of my lineage. I smell the fragrance of frankincense and vanilla in the air as these women walk with heads held high, confident in who they are. That is what I see, feel, smell. A lineage I am not explicitly connected to but know I belong. No, I am not "her." I am "*her!*" I am fierce and beautiful. Radical self-love starts from the inside out. Taylor states that it is "our inherent natural state" and we have to stop apologizing for who we are.

Update

I am still in the line waiting for a chance to get in. My conditioning is defaulting me to the line, hoping that people see me and acknowledge my value. Occasionally, I snap back to reality and

---

39   Charisse Jones and Kumea Shorter-Gooden, *Shifting: The Double Lives of Black Women in America* (Perennial, 2004). p. 60

40   Sonya Renee Taylor. *The Body is Not an Apology: The Power of Radical Self Love.* (New York: Barett-Kohler Publishers: 2021). p. 1.

ask myself, "Why am I doing this?" Why am I trying so hard to fit in?" This multigenerational conditioning is steeped into our thoughts and behavior. This is also how my leadership has evolved. A series of highs and lows; fighting the perceived images as well as the actual work of leading and supporting the educational system. As I wrestled with how to support the students in my school and district, I also wrestled with how to be seen as a competent leader in the eyes of my colleagues.

A notable example of the internal/external conflict was the nomination hearing of Judge Ketanji Brown Jackson, the first Black woman nominated to the Supreme Court. Just as I watched Anita Hill questioned in the Clarence Thomas sexual harassment case, I watched Judge Jackson endure extreme and unwanted scrutiny of qualifications even though she has the most impressive job experience of the most recent appointees since the confirmation of Justice Sotomayor. Senator Ted Cruz repeatedly displayed excerpts from children's books about race, particularly Ibram X. Kendi's book, *Antiracist Baby*, and asked her about her beliefs related to the book. This had nothing to do with her record nor her legal decisions as a public defender. There were moments in the interrogations when you visibly see her frustration with the questioning and feel the hurt that this was a tactic to discredit her years of service and love for this country. A pivotal point in the hearing came when Senator Cory Booker from New Jersey used his thirty minutes to praise Judge Jackson for her "grit and grace." He stated, "I've just watched you, with dignity and grace, field what I can only imagine is behind those questions - this doubt that is being sown." He then added, "You've earned this spot. You are worthy." Judge Jackson wiped away tears because in that moment Black women understood those words very deeply. Worthiness is the act or quality of being enough. Even the most decorated women in leadership struggle with worthiness. This is what I am fighting for in myself and within my leadership—to be full, to be enough. And, yet at times, I relapse.

These lapses are not meant to discourage me but remind me that I am a work in progress. The struggle is real! What if we can be free from this space and live in the moment as our authentic selves? I am longing for that freedom, and I am getting closer each day. Recovery, rediscovery, and self-love require the undoing of decades of "in-between" living and suit and mask-wearing. I know that it will not take a few days, weeks, or even a few years to undo this, but I am declaring that I will stop apologizing for being who I am. I am on the path of reclaiming my soul, the soul dressed in bright hues, sparkling with melanated skin, and fragrant with frankincense and vanilla.

Questions to ponder as you become unwrapped:

1. What are you constantly navigating?
2. What are the coping mechanisms you use to "survive"?
3. What do you long for when it comes to your authentic self? What would you look like? Feel like? Smell like?
4. What is your comfortable outfit?
5. What is stopping you from wearing it every day?
6. What can you do differently to reduce the "weight"?
7. What are you willing to do differently?

Strategies and tools you already know. (**Now use them with a different lens**)

- Gather your tribe. Find positive people who empower you, tell you the truth, and lift you when you fall.

- Learn your history. Read books, watch/listen to videos and podcasts, research the data, and attend virtual or in-person workshops and seminars related to gender and race.
  - Books/articles to get you started:
    - *Hood Feminism*
    - "Say Her Name: Resisting Police Brutality Against Black Women"
    - *How to be an Antiracist*
    - *The Fix*
    - *Untamed*
    - *The Gift of Imperfection*
    - *The Body is Not an Apology: The Power of Radical Self-Love*
    - *We Want to Do More Than Survive: Abolitionist Teaching and the Pursuit of Educational Freedom*
    - *Shifting Based on the African American Women's Voices Project: The Double Lives of Black Women in America*

- Love yourself. List all of the things you *love* about yourself. If you need help, ask a friend, spouse, parent, child, and so on. Start there and then lean into those characteristics. Watch the Ted Talk, "The Danger of a Single Story," by Chimamanda Ngozi Adichie

- Be inclusive. Consider the overlap of identity and oppression. This requires us to view others as more than just a single category. Be open and listen to learn and understand.

- Practice. Practice being your real you in front of strangers. Try it on!

THRIVING WOMEN

Thriving (n.)—prospering or realizing a goal despite or because of circumstances.

HISTORY IS FILLED with stories of women thriving despite or because of circumstances. What does not get told are the stories of the deep pain, trauma, and sacrifices that these women have made to move us where we are today. We honor these women as we stand on their shoulders. For some, even after death, they are carrying the heavy load of their legacy as women continue to fight for equity and voice. As we are writing this book, we have witnessed the first woman and woman of color inaugurated as vice president of the United States, and the first Black woman appointed to the Supreme Court. We witnessed the beauty in the words of Amanda Gorman, the first young poet laureate to speak at an inauguration, who asks in her opening recitation, "When day comes we ask ourselves, where can we find light in this never-ending shade?" And she answered with, "For there is always light, if only we're brave enough to see it. If only we're brave enough to be it."

What we have learned, through our experiences and in writing this book, is that we have to be courageous in our quest to change the narrative for women in leadership. Courage is a leadership move!

And yes, it comes with risks. You will be battered and bruised, but this is the only way to emerge into the light from the arena. Brené Brown conceptualized the fear that stops us from stepping into the arena: self-doubt, shame, uncertainty, comparison, and anxiety. These are the very emotions and self-talk that prevent us from fully realizing all the goals we set for ourselves, showing up wholly in our strengths, and creating the life we most desire. And we want it to be easy. It won't always be easy. But we can normalize feeling those opposing emotions at the same time.

One of the most famous Audre Lorde's quotes says, "When we speak we are afraid our words will not be heard nor welcomed, but when we are silent we are still afraid, so it is better to speak." This project has allowed us both to walk deeply into our stories, face our fears, and lay out what we want for ourselves and other women. We courageously explored our own socialization. We scrutinized expectations placed upon us by family and society and searched for new ways of showing up. We have and continue to learn new ways of expressing our needs, hopes, fears, and deepest desires. We are creating healthy boundaries. Our hope for you and for all women leaders is to have the experience of not just surviving but being alive.

It is not easy to walk into your story. Shoot, it took me several years to attempt to write mine. I didn't want to upset anyone, cause discomfort. I wanted to keep the peace. It's easier that way. But what I realized was that it's easier for everyone else but me. My peacekeeping benefited others and only served to silence, isolate, and keep me small. No more. I choose to cause that constructive discomfort. I choose to become unwrapped from all that was binding me.

I want my efforts to result in the unheard being heard and the unseen being seen. I don't want to just disrupt for the sake of disruption. I want to see more women, especially Black women, and all women who have been silenced and marginalized, rise to senior-level leadership positions in schools and districts, remain there for as long as they desire, and thrive. That means we need new language, new skill sets, to create allies, accomplices, and coconspirators. Just like Senator Duckworth and Senator Klobuchar did for one another. We need to understand our strengths and how to use them. And we need to know, truly know, that no matter what happens we are enough.

We do so much teaching now on emotional awareness and literacy with students. Are we doing the same for adults? We need to teach leaders, and not just women, on campus, and in the school building how to offload emotions in a healthy way. I remained silent because I was too afraid to speak up. I remained silent because it was too uncomfortable and scary to call out the bad behavior of others. I remained silent because I thought it was best to keep my emotions under control. I was concerned and afraid of how I might be labeled as a woman with emotions. We must learn our emotions are not binary. We can be scared, brave, anxious, bold all at the same time.

So, where do we go from here? This is a process, and we are not aiming for perfection. But we are striving to live a life worth fighting for—equitable, flourishing, enriching, empowering, and authentic. We are trying to model the awesomely flawed and courageous journey that we're taking to find space for women in educational leadership to thrive. We know that we stand on the shoulders of a myriad of women who have paved the way for us to do our work, and we honor their courage and sacrifice. That is why we won't stop, even when it is hard.

Dr. Bettina L. Love sums up a way of leading and educating that transforms us as activists and justice seekers. Love describes a "life of exhaustion, a life of doubt, a life of state-sanctioned violence, and a life consumed with the objective of surviving."[41] She also states that survival is not the goal, but the goal must be "pursuing freedom at all costs as a collective group of abolitionist-minded people who welcome struggle."[42]

This is where people tend to stop their progress, at the struggle. Struggle, failure, hurt, sacrifice, are all part of the journey. They are also part of learning and growing. As educators, parents, and a society, we have lauded success and perfectionism and admonished failure. We are a society of "everyone gets a trophy" and forget that the lessons are in losing, failure, and struggle. We are learning our greatest lessons from our struggles, and this is where the thriving begins.

Now, the main objective of this book is to open your eyes to who you are, how you have navigated your personal and professional space, and how the navigation has influenced your decisions as an educational leader. This is a monumental first step in the learning process. The next part is taking what you have learned and improving your leadership, your environment, and your future.

Kendra

I am gaining the courage. I am still holding on to the mindset of waiting it out because I am scared to death! The person getting in the way is me. I know it.

My husband is constantly saying, "Kendra, you want your cake and eat it, too."

And I reply, "Aren't you supposed to eat the cake if given?"

I want my cake, and I want to eat it. I do not want to *give up* something, but I know that my reality may require me to *give* some-

---

41   *We Want to Do More than Survive*, p. 39
42   Ibid, p. 161

thing. The "what ifs" are loud in my head. What if I fail? What if I am not good enough? What if this move will set my family back financially? Ugh! See, this creeps in all the time. Moving from surviving to thriving is not an easy task. I know it is necessary for my overall well-being, but courage over comfort is hard. That is why I am not advising but simply sharing that the struggle is *real*.

There are times at work when I feel like I am supposed to take the shit so that others after me can have an easier time. That is what was prepared for me. Others sacrificed so that I can enjoy some of the access and opportunities that were not afforded in the past. That is true and also the rationale I use to stay put. But taking the shit makes you feel like shit. Is this the example I am supposed to set?

"Hey, ladies! Take the shit!"

"It's your rite of passage!"

No. This is part of the "in-between" that I continue to navigate as well. This is an internal battle I wage. The most courageous battle I am facing is with myself. I am weighing what I should do next in my leadership journey. So, what do I do? I learn. I joined a collective. I write. I speak. I seek coconspirators who I lean on to help me gain the courage to make my next move. I am getting there.

And I know that there is never a right time. It will just be time. I feel it in my bones. Every day, I am inching closer to something else.

Here is what I am thinking:

1. I want to be a historical discussionist—a person who facilitates discussions about historical experiences over a cooked meal. I will call it "A Mouthful Vacation Experience." The best stories are shared over a plate of well-seasoned soul food and a stiff drink. This is how I learned the stories of my history, the lessons of survival, and the ways to navigate the world as a Black woman. My family continues the tradition today of

telling stories, sharing black and white photos, and preparing a favorite family dish. In fact, our family has been featured in a few food magazines highlighting our feasts and stories. This is in my DNA. This is how I love to commune and learn.

2. I want to coach women in educational leadership. I want women to think about their leadership moves, how they support and design schools for all children, and how they create spaces for staff, students, and families to learn their history, their place in it, and how they can positively contribute to the future of society for all, especially marginalized people. Coaching is my passion. From the time I was a basketball player through my career as an educator, I have valued the impact of coaching. Because I believe that people are innate learners, coaching provides an intimate and reflective way of learning about who you are so that you can invest in your talents.

3. I want to live in a small cottage near a lake or beach and sell ice cream. I want to live a simple life where I meet people, learn who they are, and engage in meaningful discussion over a sweet treat. I love the water. As a kid, my grandmother, great-grandmother, and great-aunts took my brother and me to Atlantic City every summer. Some of my best memories were hanging out with my elders and learning their ways as we played on the beach. Before I got married, Jason and I had our first vacation in the Bahamas. I learned I was pregnant with my second child, Justice, on Jones Beach in New York (and that is for another story). Now that Jason and I are parents, we have started our own family tradition by taking a yearly family trip to Cancun, Mexico. These vacations are when I am the freest. I have

clarity when I hear the waves from the ocean and taste the hint of salt on my pallet. Near water is the place where I feel the most at peace.

Now, these three "moves" seem so random and unrelated. But they make perfect sense to me. I want to talk! I want to engage in meaningful and rich conversations with people without judgment. I want to learn how and why people think about things. I want to dig deep into what drives people with the hope that they also learn about me. This is how I will thrive. Getting there means letting go of some of my comforts or what I believe may be disguised as comforts. If they were truly comforts, then I would not feel the pull to do one or all of the three things I listed. Huh!

Even as I am writing this, I am conflicted. My tribe, my husband, mother, best friend, and trusted colleagues are rooting for me, encouraging me to leap, but my modus operandi is to create a plan and follow it. This is how I was conditioned to move. Plan and execute. Never do anything spontaneous and reduce any risk. The plan I was developing and following was charted for me, based on a series of cautious moves I made to reduce the hurt, follow the rules of engagement, and climb the rungs of the success ladder. All the while, I tried to bury the idea that these rules were laden with White, male-dominated ideas and rules.

Again, if I just worked hard, kept my head down, and forged ahead, I would be successful, happy, and most of all—accepted. I have come to realize that no matter what course of action I take, leadership requires risk. You see, leadership is courage, and courage is uncomfortable. Discomfort makes you move. So, to thrive, you have to experience discomfort.

This discomfort comes from understanding how we have been led and how we have been trained to educate and lead. As I reflect on my training, I realize that much of the formal training was steeped in a male-dominated western ideology of leadership. As I tried to fit into the schema, I immediately felt like it did not fit but brushed it off as the hard work of leadership. I wrapped myself in this thinking, and it was uncomfortable from the start, but I didn't know better or see clearly that there was something amiss.

This training was juxtaposed with the informal training and life lessons of the bold Black women in my life who urged me to speak up, dare greatly, and change the world. These two worlds often collide, leading me to the state of the "in-between." What I have come to learn is that the formal leadership training construct is not natural for me as a Black woman. My frame includes the intersection of race and gender which leads to a different type of leadership—reflective, passionate, empowering, sensitive, and equitable.

I am not saying that men cannot exhibit these qualities. I am saying that understanding what it means through the eyes of a woman in leadership requires a level of resilience, persistence, patience, and vision. That is because we have to navigate male-dominated spaces differently, especially as 84% of our companies are led by men, and in educational leadership, only 13.7 percent of superintendents are women.[43] Glass states that some of the factors contributing to few women in the superintendency include women being poorly positioned for the role, poor recruitment efforts, lack of credentials, personal preferences, and the glass ceiling. These factors and a variety of others are indicative of issues facing women in leadership in multiple industries.

Women are overrepresented in the service, hospitality, healthcare, and education sectors at entry-level and some mid-level positions, but as you move up the ladder of leadership, the stark

43   Thomas E. Glass, "Where Are All the Women Superintendents." (The School Administrator, 2000) https://aasa.org/schooladministratorarticle.aspx?id=14492

absence of their presence is alarming. There is the assumed idea that women are hard workers, can take care of the day-to-day operations, and interact with consumers/customers, but they are not capable of leading the organization. Leave that to the men who know and can do better. When you peel away the perceived logic that has riddled the industry, you can see how absurd it is. Women make up over 70 percent of the teachers in the classrooms and entry manager positions in the central office, and the number of women serving as local school principals has increased, but the number of women of color has remained nearly unchanged.

According to the National Center for Educational Statistics (NCES), the percentage of public-school principals who were female in 2017–18 (54 percent) was 10 percentage points higher than in 1999–2000 (44 percent). The number of Black principals remained at 11 percent while the number of Hispanic principals increased by 4 percent.[44] These statistics offer a backdrop to the experiences that women and women of color may face as they attempt to lead in our public educational systems.

First, there is the possibility of isolation. With very few colleagues who can relate to the job stressors, work environment, and lived experiences, the job can be very lonely and unsatisfying. This isolation can lead to an environment of exclusionary tactics with micro or macro aggressions. As Tonya Echols explains in her 2020 *Forbes* article "Leading While Black: Leading during the Racial Injustice Awakening," she has often been whitesplained about Black issues or been expected to answer questions on behalf of the Black population. What is most poignant about her article is her statement that "society perpetuates the shadow set of rules that many

---

44   "Characteristics of Public School Principals," Coe - characteristics of Public School Principals, 2020, https://nces.ed.gov/programs/coe/indicator/cls.

Black people live with, not by choice but for survival."[45] And the intersection of gender and race compounds and complicates the rules even more.

How do you move from surviving to thriving? In fact, I must quote two Harvard professors, Martin Linsky and Ronald Heifetz, who state, "Leadership is an improvisational art. You may have an overarching vision, clear, orienting values, and even a strategic plan, but what you actually do from moment to moment cannot be scripted. To be effective, you must respond to what is happening."[46] They also say, "Exercising leadership is an expression of your aliveness. But when you cover yourself up, you risk losing something as well. In the struggle to save yourself, you can give up too many of those qualities that are the essence of being alive, like innocence, curiosity, and compassion."[47]

I know! I am quoting two White men from Harvard, and they are right. How this shows up for me and how people respond as Black women can be exhausting, frustrating, and risky. This is my reality and that of many others who are looking for answers. The story I shared about my upbringing, my education, and my leadership screams for the "expression of my aliveness." I have been yearning for it over the years. I have had glimpses of it. But that yearning is increasing and reaching a fever pitch.

When I get a taste of it, it feels natural, and as Glennon Doyle describes, untamed and free. I am not advocating that to thrive or feel free, you have to have positional power (that would be great, if so), but I recommend that you take stock in how you have been navigating your leadership journey, paying attention to what

---

45   Tonya Echols, "Council Post: Leading While Black: Leadership during the Racial Injustice Awakening," Forbes (Forbes Magazine, July 20, 2020).

46   Ronald A. Heifitz and Marty Linsky, *Leadership on the Line* (Boston, MA: Harvard Business Review Press, 2002).

47   Ibid, 119.

excites you and what gives you energy. What have you been firing on all cylinders? What helps you energize others you lead? Are you wrapped in your authenticity or are you still needing to unwrap years of otherness? I am advocating for a state of being that transcends position and yet helps you inspire the people you lead to be better. So, how can you thrive as a woman educational leader?

1. Know your passion and act on it as much as possible. Brené Brown tells us that we have to be realistic with our courageous and daring leadership. We are not saying that you have to abandon your current life and work and jump feet first into your next passion. Maybe you can, if you have the means. We recommend that you "touch it" often. I love to coach people, and I find a variety of ways to support the development of people, especially women. I visit schools, talk to leaders on my ride home from work, listen to podcasts, participate in a monthly book study primarily led and attended by women in leadership, and attend numerous professional learning sessions related to leadership development and equity. I keep my passion for coaching and development close to me. I love to talk to people and understand how they tick. I am a people watcher and love to learn the story of people, especially those who lead. Keep your passion close so that when you decide to go all in, you are ready.

2. Encourage and support each other. We know that there can be stiff competition among women when there are only a few open positions for leadership but rooting for each other and providing support will help encourage women in leadership to persist, even amid unrelenting scrutiny. This is why we must build each other up versus adding to the din of can'ts and don'ts.

3. Show up for each other. Be present for your sisters and show up authentically. As you have learned and from the first-hand experience, there are already barriers to access and opportunities for women in leadership. Your presence, allyship, and coconspiratorship will create a network of women who will speak up and speak out in the face of micro and macro aggressions. Our sisters need us to take them from being in the corner to the seat of the table. During the summer of 2020, I wanted to find a way to speak out and up more broadly for the women who have been silenced, dismissed, and pressured to stay in the perceived place. That was the impetus for T-Shirt Statement Saturday and #tshirt-statement. In addition, I follow #SayHerName which raised the awareness of the number of Black girls and women who have been victimized by police violence. Their stories are often missing from the mainstream media or the narrative about the victimization of the Black woman. Breonna Taylor, Sandra Bland, Eleanor Bumpers, India Kager, and countless others' stories are untold. These women were daughters, mothers, citizens, and humans. They were also our students with the promise of the American dream. How will you give voice to the girls and women you lead?

4. Acknowledge and cultivate talent. When you see someone who has the potential to lead, encourage her and provide her with opportunities to lead. The best thing you can do to support women in leadership is to help to build the capacity of others. Avoid coveting what you learn, or you will become complicit in the thickening of the glass ceiling we all are trying to break. When you see a student or teacher who has the leadership potential, coach them by learning

who they are and what they are passionate about. Be careful not to guide them in fitting in. Help them discover their strengths and find ways to foster these talents to support the positive impact on the lives of the students they partner with or serve. If you do not have the confidence or skill to do this, connect them with someone who does. If talent is not fostered, women on the leadership journey will burn out, become discouraged, or diminish their talents.

5. Have a plan. Of course, I had to add this one. This is part of my conditioning. I am not recommending that you have a "Kendra" plan but know what it is that you want for yourself, the environment that will foster your talents, and the type of people who will encourage, support, and advocate for you. Be able to answer the questions, "Who are you and what do you do?" As a leader, you will need a mentor or coach who can keep you grounded and help you navigate the work. This goes back to having your tribe, your people who will interrogate your plan and let you know if you are off course, unclear, or in dangerous territory. Now, there is a caveat to this recommendation. The plan you create is grounded in your personal, professional vision and moral imperative. And you have to get this right. During my leadership journey, I had some missteps, and I wavered a bit from the path. And that is all right because I am unlearning, learning, and growing. So, the first step of the plan starts with knowing yourself.

6. Lead. This seems like an obvious recommendation, right? In our roles as leaders, we have to be reminded to lead. Take the first step, be daring, and model the way. Here is the scary and awesome work of leadership. All eyes are

on us. People are watching our every move to determine how they should think and act. So, if we want to create school environments where administrators, teachers, and students feel that they belong, are authentic, can critically think, question, investigate, and seek feedback, then we have to model this behavior in all that we do personally and professionally.

Kelly

What's my next move? I no longer want to keep the peace. At least not in the way that extinguishes me and my voice. I no longer want to be afraid to speak up for what I think, feel, or need in fear of what others might think or the way it might make them feel. I don't believe everything needs to be presented as a pretty package. Perfect is no longer my benchmark. People and life are messy. I need to let it be messy.

I want to make a difference for women leaders and especially for women leaders who for way too long have been silenced, marginalized, and told they need to be "fixed". I want to be a coconspirator, not just an ally. I no longer want to sit in spaces where we simply talk about what's happening to us. Rather, I want to create brave spaces where women leaders can learn, plan, and strategize how to transform systems and create brave and healthy cultures. And I want to be active. Active! Not just talk about the need to change but to truly be the change. I want to become unwrapped. Together.

1. I want to build Daring Women Leader Communities: I want to use my certification as a Dare to Lead™ facilitator to create communities in all school districts of daring women

leaders. I want to support women along their daring leadership journey and help them sustain this work in order to stay the course and not default back to what is easy. I want to help break those patterns of behavior and replace them with ones that serve us better.

2. I, too, want to executive coach women leaders. Women need brave spaces to come to and offload emotions, unpack daily experiences, try out new ways of being, and ask complicated questions in order to seek uncomplicated answers. I want to use my coaching training to support women educators in order to increase the number of women in senior-level leadership positions in schools, districts, and campuses.

3. I want to create a permanent brave space for women leaders. I, like Kendra, love the water. I want to live and work near water. I am most at peace and feel more like myself when I am near a lake. My happy place is sitting on a deck, porch, or dock watching the sunrise and fall over the water. I want to create that same space for women leaders to create, learn, rest, reenergize and support one another. I want to establish a women's education leadership retreat near water. I will be in search of that lakeside retreat.

Are our goals, plans, and desires big and audacious? Maybe. But why not? We no longer want to live or play small. So, there you have it. What is wrapped up is now unraveling. We are going forth to start this new journey together, helping each other unpeel each layer while attending to our wounds and sharing the care and leadership women want and need.

Kendra and Kelly

Thank you for reading! We hope that our experiences and our own self-discovery inspire you to learn more about yourself and others who are experiencing their own journeys. For our sisters, the world needs our brilliance and our whole selves. Look at our legacy of resilience, strength, and beauty. Imagine what we can do together! For our partners, we need you! We need you to stand up for us and use your voice and actions to eradicate the inequities in our education system that unfairly marginalize girls, women, and women of color.

The incomparable bell hooks says "I want there to be a place in the world where people can engage in one another's differences in a way that is redemptive, full of hope and possibility."[48] That is what we hope for - a place where we stand shoulder to shoulder, in community, in love, barely our authentic selves. Until then, we will continue to pursue justice, live and love for good, build a community of sisterhood, and improve the presence of thriving women in educational leadership.

---

48   hooks, bell. 1996 Reel to Real: Race, Sex, and Class at the Movies pg 122

BIBLIOGRAPHY

"Black Women & The Pay Gap." AAUW, September 14, 2021. https://www.aauw.org/resources/article/Black-women-and-the-pay-gap/.

Bray, Rosemary. "Taking Sides Against Ourselves." *The New York Times*. November 17, 1991.

"Characteristics of Public School Principals." COE - Characteristics of Public School Principals, 2020. https://nces.ed.gov/programs/coe/indicator/cls.

Calderwood , Imogen, and Erica Sánchez. "There's Finally an Internationally Agreed upon Definition of Sexism. Here's Why That Matters." Global Citizen, April 2019. https://www.globalcitizen.org/en/content/sexism-definition-council-of-europe-equality/#:~:text=Sexism%20is%20defined%20as%3A%20%E2%80%9CAny,%2C%20whether%20online%20or%20offline.%E2%80%9D.

Crenshaw, Kimberle. "Demarginalizing the Intersection of Race and Sex: A Black Feminist Critique of Antidiscrimination Doctrine, Feminist Theory and Antiracist Politics." University of Chicago Legal Forum, 1989. https://chicagounbound.uchicago.edu/cgi/viewcontent.cgi?article=1052&context=uclf.

"DeGraffenreid v. General Motors Assembly Div., Etc., 413 F. Supp. 142 (E.D. Mo. 1976)." Justia Law. Accessed January 29, 2022. https://law.justia.com/cases/federal/district-courts/FSupp/413/142/1660699/.

Doyle, Glennon. *Untamed.* New York, NY: The Dial Press, 2020.

Echols, Tonya. "Council Post: Leading While Black: Leadership during the Racial Injustice Awakening." Forbes. Forbes Magazine, July 20, 2020. https://www.forbes.com/sites/forbescoachescouncil/2020/07/21/leading-while-Black-leadership-during-the-racial-injustice-awakening/?sh=5b0291b76e23.

Elliott, G., Suzanne Kao, and A. Grant. "Mattering: Empirical Validation of a Social-Psychological Concept: Semantic Scholar." Self & Identity, 2004. https://www.semanticscholar.org/paper/Mattering%3A-Empirical-Validation-of-a-Concept-Elliott-Kao/2eef461c045e1044c767e5367147eff430db5a10.

Facio, Alda. "What Is Patriarchy? - Learnwhr.org." Women's Human Rights Institute, 2013. http://www.learnwhr.org/wp-content/uploads/D-Facio-What-is-Patriarchy.pdf.

Freire, Paulo *Pedagogy of the Oppressed.* New York: Penguin, 2017.

Gandhi, Vipula and Jennifer Robison. "Wellbeing Stats for Women in the Workplace Show a Need for Change." Gallup.com. Gallup, July 23, 2021. https://www.gallup.com/workplace/352529/wellbeing-stats-women-workplace-show-need-change.aspx.

Grant, Adam. "Perspective | Who Won't Shut up in Meetings? Men Say It's Women. It's Not." The Washington Post. WP Company, February 18, 2021. https://www.washingtonpost.com/outlook/2021/02/18/men-interrupt-women-tokyo-olympics/.

Glass, Thomas E. "Where Are All the Women Superintendents." *The School Administrator 57* (2000): 28-32.

Harter, James K., Frank L. Schmidt, Sangeeta Agrawal, and Stephanie K. Plowman. The Relationship Between Engagement at Work And Organizational Outcomes. Gallup, February 2013. https://employeeengagement.com/wp-content/uploads/2013/04/2012-Q12-Meta-Analysis-Research-Paper.pdf.

Heifitz, Ronald A., and Marty Linsky. *Leadership on the Line.* Boston, MA: Harvard Business Review Press, 2002.

hooks, bell. *Reel to Real: Race, Sex, and Class at the Movies.* outledge, 1996.

Jones, Charisse, and Kumea Shorter-Gooden. *Shifting: The Double Lives of Black Women in America.* Perennial, 2004.

Kendi, Ibram X. *How to Be an Antiracist.* New York: One World, 2019.

Love, Bettina. *We Want to Do More than Survive: Abolitionist Teaching and the Pursuit of Educational Freedom*. Beacon, 2020.

Madgavkar, Anu, Olivia White, Mekala Krishnan, Deepa Mahajan, and Xavier Azcue. "Covid-19 and Gender Equality: Countering the Regressive Effects." McKinsey & Company. McKinsey & Company, April 10, 2021. https://www.mckinsey.com/featured-insights/future-of-work/covid-19-and-gender-equality-countering-the-regressive-effects.

Maranto, Robert, Robert Maranto Kristen Carroll Albert Cheng Manuel P. Teodoro Rachel S. White, Joshua P. Starr, et al. "Boys Will Be Superintendents: School Leadership as a Gendered Profession ." kappanonline.org, October 3, 2018. https://kappanonline.org/maranto-carroll-cheng-teodoro-school-leadership-gender/.

Michals, Debra, ed. "Sojourner Truth." Biography: Sojourner truth. National Women's History Museum, 2015. https://www.womenshistory.org/education-resources/biographies/sojourner-truth.

Neff, Kristin. *Fierce Self-Compassion: How Women Can Harness Kindness to Speak up, Claim Their Power, and. Thrive*. New York, NY: Harper Wave, 2021.

Parker, Priya. *The Art of Gathering: How We Meet and Why It Matters*. Penguin USA, 2020.

Scott, Susan. *Fierce Conversations: Achieving Success at Work and in Life, One Conversation at a Time*. London, UK: Piatkus, 2017.

"Speech Entitled 'Ain't i a Woman?' - the Hermitage." Accessed January 29, 2022. https://thehermitage.com/wp-content/uploads/2016/02/Sojourner-Truth_Aint-I-a-Woman_1851.pdf.

"The Proclamation." Sisters Testify. Accessed March 3, 2022. https://www.sisterstestify.com/about/the-proclamation/.

ABOUT THE AUTHORS

 **KENDRA WASHINGTON-BASS, PHD** is an educational leader, speaker, and facilitator who coaches and develops school leaders. She is also an expert in the design of principal and school leadership pipelines. She serves on a number of boards and organizations supporting leadership development in civic and educational sectors.

 **KELLY PEAKS HORNER, MED** is a trained and certified executive education leadership and culture coach. She is a Dare to Lead™ facilitator who teaches courageous leadership skills based on the research of Dr. Brené Brown. With over thirty-five years of experience in the education sector, she works to disrupt systems so all within them may thrive.